MORALITY
& POWER

Contemporary Jewish Views

Edited by

Daniel J. Elazar

RSITY
S OF
RICA

Lanham • New York • London

THE JERUSALEM CENTER FOR
PUBLIC AFFAIRS

Copyright © 1990 by

The Jerusalem Center for Public Affairs

University Press of America®, Inc.

4720 Boston Way
Lanham, MD 20706

3 Henrietta Street
London WC2E 8LU England

British Cataloging in Publication Information Available

Co-published by arrangement with
The Jerusalem Center for Public Affairs

Managing Editor: Mark Ami-El
Typesetting: Custom Graphics and Publishing Ltd., Jerusalem

Library of Congress Cataloging-in-Publication Data

Morality and power : contemporary Jewish views /
edited by Daniel J. Elazar.
p.   cm.
"The Jerusalem Center for Public Affairs."
1. Jewish–Arab relations—Moral and ethical aspects.   2. Israel—
Moral conditions.   3. West Bank—History—Palestinian
Uprising, 1987–   .   4. Gaza Strip—History—
Palestinian Uprising, 1987–   .   I. Elazar, Daniel Judah.
II. Merkaz ha–Yerushalmi le– inyene tsibur u–medinah.
DS119.7.M645   1989   305.8'0095694'09048—dc20   89–39021 CIP

ISBN 0–8191–7608–7
ISBN 0–8191–7609–5 (pbk.)

THE MILKEN LIBRARY OF JEWISH PUBLIC AFFAIRS

Made possible by a gift from the
Milken Family Foundation

CONTENTS

v

INTRODUCTION

Daniel J. Elazar

In September 1988, as the *intifada* approached the end of its first year, the Jerusalem Center for Public Affairs invited a distinguished group of leaders in academic and public affairs in Israel and the diaspora to participate in a symposium on the problems of relating morality and power in contemporary statecraft. We asked participants to respond to three questions:

1) Is there a difference between individual morality and the morality of public policy choices for a state or other political community?

2) Assuming a less than perfect world, how should political communities, their leaders and members deal with the problem of maintaining moral positions under duress or at times of crisis?

3) To what extent does or should a morally relativistic or morally absolutist position influence one's conclusions with regard to the first two questions?

We initiated the symposium for three reasons. The immediate one was the spate of callow and superficial moral criticisms of Israel on the part of the mass media covering events in the territories, joined by the reactions of "anguished" professional Jewish moralists, principally but not exclusively in the diaspora, as well as the usual critics of Israel who exploited the. opportunity to the hilt. We at the Jerusalem Center came to the conclusion that whatever the rights and wrongs of the intifada itself, we could not leave the moral field to those self-proclaimed moral arbiters.

Beyond that, the decade of the 1980s has seen an erosion of Israel's moral position in the world for real or imagined reasons. The political consequences of that erosion are clear to behold, both in the form of new challenges to Israel's position abroad and in increasing divisiveness and loss of self-confidence at home.

There is also the larger question of the relationship between morality and power which confronts every polity in determining its policies and actions and which we as Jews must fully confront once again as a result of our return to statehood. Those of us who have argued that the reestablishment of the State of Israel is not only morally challenging but enables Jews to test the norms of

1

their civilization and the premises of their faith in the most concrete and practical ways, must engage in consideration of the issues of morality and power as they are played out in the life and actions of the Jewish state and must seek to develop guidelines for Israeli and Jewish public policy through the most serious inquiry into the question. We view this symposium as a step in that direction.

The symposium itself grows out of that special combination of concern for the Jewish political tradition and the contemporary Jewish public agenda which is characteristic of our Center and has been the focal point of its work. Many of the contributors have been involved in that effort as Fellows, Associates or Overseers of the Jerusalem Center or members of one of its workshops. Others have not. Nevertheless, the responses of all are consciously Jewish and deliberately rest upon — and usually explicitly refer to — Jewish sources, beginning with the Bible. In most cases they felicitously combine this Jewish grounding with a consideration of the concerns and works of Western political philosophy. Thus we find Machiavelli contrasted with Bahya ibn Pakuda, Hillel the Elder linked with Emanuel Kant, and *halakhah* weighed in connection with the principles of natural law and justice. In that respect this symposium is potentially a significant contribution to political thought, dealing as it does with a universal question from a perspective that is at once universal and appropriately rooted in the concrete situation of a concrete people.

Our authors move back and forth between the general and the specific, interweaving the two just as they interweave Jewish and general sources. The end result is that, within a wide spectrum of viewpoints presented by people of varying backgrounds and vocations, cutting across much of the political spectrum — left, right, and center — we have a near consensus that fits squarely within the mainstream of Jewish political thought. There is general agreement on the existence of absolute moral parameters, binding public as well as private behavior, states as well as individuals, but with much room for consequential moral decisions within those parameters, more for states than for individuals. Moreover, there is a general consensus that moral decisions require serious consideration of ends and means, with certain highly moral ends justifying means which if taken alone would be of questionable morality, while at the same time certain means are too immoral to be considered, even for the best ends.

Throughout all of the contributions, with a few exceptions, runs a strong rejection of oversimplification. This effort to avoid over-simplification unites people whose conclusions with regard to the specific problems of Israel and the *intifada* and in relation to the Palestinian Arabs are very different indeed. It is what makes this symposium a dialogue in which people talk to one another from within a common moral understanding rather than separately or past one another. This is reflected in the way in which there are overlapping references in the essays although none of the participants saw those of any of the others.

There is a frequent recurrence to the teachings of Machiavelli, sometimes with approval, sometimes through explication, and sometimes in rejection. The dilemmas of Abraham Lincoln and the American Civil War receive their share of attention, as does Franklin Delano Roosevelt's incarceration of Japanese Americans at the beginning of World War II. But within those parameters there is a vigorous discussion which tends to meet in the middle around such basic Jewish political principles as legitimacy of national self-expression, the necessity for developing the world community as a community of nations, the need to wrestle with moral questions in the exercise of power, and the moral dignity that striving brings to human actions, even when human behavior is inevitably flawed.

In this the Bible particularly and *halakhic* sources secondarily play a major role for most of the participants, whether they lean toward religious Orthodoxy or religious liberalism. Nor is Scripture quoted as proof test as is often the case in theological discussions of these questions. Rather it is searched for political teachings the way it should be. Only when some of our political analysts slide over into a homiletic posture do they sometimes violate this consensus. Abraham, Joseph and his brothers, Moses, Joshua, Jeptha, and Samuel provide us with hard teachings about the relationship between morality and power according to our essayists, most of whom remain "hard-nosed" throughout.

The participants are a varied group. Seven are Israelis and fourteen Americans. Seven are political scientists by training and four others are political philosophers or political commentators whose background was originally in other disciplines. Six have published in the field of Jewish political studies. Other academic disciplines represented are economics, history, law and sociology. Six are political activists. One is a Jewish communal worker. Two others are Jewish communal leaders. One was a judge, one was a member of the United States Cabinet, and another occupies a similar position in Israel. Five are rabbis including leading figures in the three mainstream branches of contemporary Judaism.

What can we conclude from all this? There is clear agreement that nations and all but fundamentally immoral states have the right to survive and the obligation to protect the lives and security of their members or citizens. In doing so they may use appropriate methods which in themselves would not be considered moral from an absolute perspective, such as deceit and force, provided that they are used in context with appropriate humility and subject to the limitations of certain absolute moral parameters. It is generally understood that , given human flaws, mistakes will be made and excesses committed, some of which should be punished if found to be deliberate, but always with an understanding of the circumstances involved.

There is further agreement that however high the obligation of leaders of states to act to protect the lives of their citizens and those under their protection, they must also consider the lives and legitimate concerns of those whom they are confronting. Moreover, since in this imperfect world individuals may have to pay a more drastic price than do their nations or states, as for example when an individual sacrifices his life in a war to preserve his nation which, while paying a price, survives as a collectivity, that is part of the tragedy of human existence. It calls for reciprocal concern on the part of the national or state leadership to try to safeguard the members of the body politic.

While a number of the essayists hint at or clearly state their reservations about Israel's present policies, with regard to the peace-making process as a whole, and particularly with regard to the future of the territories, only one suggests that Israel is not morally justified, nay, required to preserve order in those territories as long as it is responsible for them. Indeed, even those who do not want Israel to retain permanent control over the territories make their argument on prudential as much as on moral grounds.

The moral issues posed by Israel's situation are among the most difficult that humans confront in our time since they involve conflicting rights as well as interests and the problem of a people who were committed for nearly 4,000 years to maintaining the highest of moral standards, even when exercising political power. No symposium, nor for that matter, no philosopher can be expected to resolve these problems. What is necessary, however, is to seriously consider them on the highest plane but with an eye to the most practical application of the results of that inquiry, without abandoning either the exercise of political power or the pursuit of justice.

MORALITY: THE JEWISH NIGHTMARE

Gerald B. Bubis

The State of Israel has a dilemma. It faces the realities confronting all modern democratic states: how to act in acceptable moral terms as those standards are understood by their respective populaces. Democratic states are guided by and/or are held to account by the moral expectations of their citizens. At a given point in time private and public morality will thus result in higher or lower sets of expectations within a given population. The popular culture, taste, aesthetics, morality, teachings, and behaviors thus ebb and flow and bring with them varied rather than constant standards against which public officials and the state are measured and held accountable. These standards are also shaped by the exhortations, promises and behavior of its leaders. In short, governments both shape and are shaped by the intersecting of events, realities, opportunities, self-imposed expectations and the issues confronting them.

In that sense, Israel should be no more nor no less moral than any other given democratic state at any particular moment in history. But it is not just another modern democratic state. Its roots are embedded in a 4,000-year-long saga. It is made of the stuff of history, even as it makes history. The moral paroxysms which grip it periodically are accentuated by this past. Thus the issue of public and private morality looms larger for Israel than for other countries.

The same dilemmas can be posed for the Jewish communities of the diaspora, even though they pale in comparison to the complexities and perplexities which confront a nation-state. And in Israel's case, all these issues are exacerbated by the geo-political and military considerations confronting Israel. These are minimal expectations grounded in pragmatism and cast in no historical context.

A population today is shaped by electronic media. Issues of morality are thus as likely to find a context for judgement born of TV situation comedy and drama as they are by fine points of law, teachings or history. How else explain the phenomenon of TV bytes, the notion that in 20 seconds an issue can be delineated and

7

an answer given? How else explain an American presidential candidate invoking the immortal words of a movie character, to "make my day" as a substitute for serious discussion on the clash between individual and communal rights when discussing gun control laws?

America is not the equivalent of all that is good or lacking in the Western world. It is, however, the purveyor of mass culture and tastes to the world at large. It thus comes to personify the best and the worst of what modernity offers to the world at large. Manipulation of media can thus dull or blur moral sensibilities. Even more complicated, by ignoring issues which have profound moral complexities, the media can help people come to believe that the disappearance from view of an event is equivalent to the event never having happened. The presence of TV cameras around Sabra and Shatilla in Beirut and their absence in Hama, Syria is a case in point. The presence or absence of the witness (TV) has taught all governments a lesson which they have learned well, if at times, cynically. Control the witness and one has often won the moral battle.

Israel can no more escape the consequences of such pragmatic thinking than any other polity. All Western polities draw to greater or lesser degree upon the historic teachings of Judeo-Christian morality. Their respective permutations are shaped as a result of their own historic realities. Thus nationalism, rationalism, economic and environmental benefits and realities further shape the mythos which provide the moral teachings of each polity. Israel is thus simultaneously trapped and elevated by its own primary roots: Jewish teachings.

The Zionist dreamers, however affected by economic ideologists, revolutionary stirrings of Western Europe and other forces unique to the eighteenth, nineteenth and twentieth centuries, were seared by the teachings of the Jewish sages and prophets. The moral indignation of those teachings resonate in the world today, most often as expectations cast in absolute terms but seen as the very quintessence of how a nation-state at its best should act.

It is no accident that the Founding Fathers of the United States chose a Jewish teaching to emblazon on the Liberty Bell. A plethora of quotes could be inserted at this point to buttress the point further. Sensibility of the readers of this short essay suggests they can fill in the appropriate quotes for themselves.

Israel became, for most of the modern world, the very

apotheosis of those teachings. Here, finally, would be the political state, composed as it was primarily of the People of the Book, who would live out its collective morality at the highest level, in the Kohlbergian sense of morality. And Israel came to be the same for the Jews of the world. The "light to the world," filled with ideals and idealists, rescuing the remnants, tilling the soil, living in peace with their neighbors, declaring "liberty for all the inhabitants thereof" and living happily ever after.

The enormity of the Holocaust and the world's reaction to it confirms the sense of relativism which pervades human responses to cataclysmic events involving breaches of moral behavior. The past few years have taught the State of Israel and the Jewish people what history seems to reconfirm: there is a difference between public and private morality and behavior.

Jews have spent millennia believing in themselves as a covenanted people, a people chosen by God to do good and be good. Most Jews have been sustained by that belief even as they have sustained the belief. So has the Western world, and thus the crunch of the dilemma. Maimonides wrote about just and unjust wars when the Jews had no army. For hundreds of years before and after Maimonides the explications of the Jews' sages and rabbis were the teachings for a powerless people living in countries with powerful governments. As Israel matured it was doomed to judge itself and be judged in turn by the heightened expectations of moral behavior — a doubly imposed double standard — from within and without.

All of us who pursue the evocation of private moral behavior undoubtedly hope for a sufficient absorption of this behavior in the communities in which we live, spatially, psychologically, religiously, or by any other dimension. A recent commencement address heard by this writer reminded us of that fact. The speaker pointed out that he had learned almost all ideas and values of importance in his life in kindergarten. "Wash your hands before eating." "Look both ways before crossing the street." "Share." "Clean up after you are finished." "Be kind to your neighbor." "Be fair." "Don't take things which don't belong to you."

Philosophical pundits must know that parents for the most part raise their children to follow Micah's dictum of general behavior with humility. So what? Only to a point, and more of that later. I have higher expectations. I firmly expect for Jews and for a Jewish state that the results of being a covenanted person related to a covenanted people must be to continue to hold myself, my people, and my people's State of Israel and its leaders, accountable to a higher moral plane. I believe most Jews feel the same way.

The Jews may, as some suggest, be out of step with the world. But if that is true, what's new? Hence the dilemma and the paradox. Jews rushed headlong into modernity. They coveted its fruits and have harvested those fruits beyond most dreams. Worldwide, demonstrably, Jews have done very well materially — often at the price of morality, both individual and communal.

Our voluntary Jewish communities have empowered the economic elite with primary leadership roles in the communities. And the Jewish community needs them. Can they be imbued with moral values to the point that their public and private behavior is affected by Jewish teachings? More positives may result when those who teach are brought into the governance of our diaspora Jewish communities.

But dilemmas abound. I advocate the inclusion of rabbis and intellectuals into the voluntary governance structures of our people. Yet the bulk of the rabbis I see in governance roles in Israel are often guilty of the same excesses in their behavior which at times repel me in the diaspora. Perhaps as Israel continues to mature, its political leadership will further enhance the opportunities for voices of pluralism and diversity which will provide the counterpoint to triumphalists and messianists. Political leaders are pragmatists. Those who truly live by moral stances in times of excess are too soon most apt to be emeritus.

It is comforting to know that historically the death penalty was repugnant to our sages. It is more comforting to know that besieged Israel has to this date used the death penalty but once in its 40-year history. Yet even as these words are written, political leaders of "right" and "left" in Israel call for the death penalty for terrorists. Is this because of moral outrage or a political stance calculated to garner uncommitted voters?

In Israel the matter of moral education is at once easier and more complex than in the diaspora. In theory, Jewish teachings should permeate all school trends in Israel. The distribution of appropriate educational materials and special training for teachers should assure the greater possibility of permeating the schools and its students. Such should also be the case with TV in Israel. So? Do they?

The diaspora communities are much more problematic. The schools and communication media are shaped by many value sources and so there is little likelihood of infusion of Jewish moral teachings. The first and last redoubt remains the home, where increasing attention must be paid to these issues. As previously noted, parents and kindergarten are at one in reinforcing moral values. Such is unfortunately less frequently the case as children mature. In all societies watching what parents do is a much greater learning method than listening to what they say. In an acquisitive, materialistic society, with cynicism and fatalism more normative than hopes for redemption and social betterment, the task of moral education is daunting. Nevertheless, attempts must be made.

I therefore offer a specific suggestion which must be viewed in the larger context of a given society's true values and all the sources of reinforcement which are necessary for their actuation.

At the higher levels of the diaspora and in Israel the viability of re-covenanting must be demonstrated through a series of strategies. They must be geared to a serious review of Mordecai Kaplan's proposals related to building organic communities. The recent step of the Jerusalem Center in distributing materials on the Constitution for the State of Israel is one such concrete step. These materials, accompanied by further appropriate background materials in Israel and throughout the diaspora, might set the stage for a constitutional convention of the Jewish people.

Political and communal leaders must be engaged in this process which would have imbedded within it the moral dilemmas and case issues which arise in contemporary Jewish life. Issues ranging from the limits of self-defense, "purity of arms," to guidelines for communal fund investment, honoring donors regardless of the source of their wealth, and many other issues could be built into simulation exercises. Increased use of satellite TV and video cassettes is an inevitability. Their use must be accelerated. To capitalize on the possibilities, a series of local and regional simulation exercises could be conducted worldwide, culminating in a satellite broadcast of the exercise involving Jewish communal, legal, religious and political figures from Israel and the major diaspora communities. Curriculum materials prepared for the schools of all trends, *havurot*, parenting groups and the like, would need massive distribution. The binding of Israel and the diaspora communities might be possible if the leaders of all Jewish communities could be enlisted in the process.

This is a grandiose proposal. It will take radical action born of grandiose ideas to transcend the sleaze born of cynicism that pervades Western society today. Jews have always reflected and refracted. They have taken the best and the worst of the worlds around them. Now is the moment to take the best and reflect back the best of what Judaism teaches, in embracing, demanding, yet flexible and transcending terms.

There has never been one vision of Judaism as far as the application of its teachings is concerned. It is unlikely that pietists and pilpulists will make common cause with modernists and pluralists. Yet the call for morality will thus be answered with multiple voices and approaches. The appeal for common striving accompanied by educative tools for agreement by most would be the most one could hope for — and the healthiest approach to strive for.

These are first steps. Unshared visions as to the shared future rest upon moral premises. As this is written it is clear that not all Jews have shared visions or shared premises. We are being torn asunder by issues and concerns both external to and internal to the Jewish people.

It is not an easy time for Jews or Jewish teachings. Choices are available. For some of us Jewish moral teachings are being prostituted in the name of Jewish tradition. Voices of moderation must be accompanied with an action agenda which will help the Jewish people seek the healthiest paths to living, drawing upon moral Jewish teachings through education and reason.

THE ONLY ABSOLUTE GROUND OF PUBLIC MORALITY IS THE VISION, HUMANITY, AND UNSENTIMENTAL PRUDENCE OF LEADERSHIP

Joseph Cropsey

It is clear that the choices faced by an individual differ by orders of magnitude from those faced by the government of a state. An individual is responsible for his own well-being and for that of his family and to some extent his friends. To state, as is sometimes done, that each man is responsible for all of mankind is to speak without meaning or to declaim a sentiment as if it were a thought. The man who has the responsibility for his and his family's well-being must indeed have a conviction about the significance of "well-being," or good, but if he is mistaken, vague or corrupt in that conviction, the harm that he can do is necessarily limited. The leadership of a state carries a burden of responsibility that is vastly greater, not by virtue merely of the number of human lives affected by its acts but by virtue also of the nature of the influence that the existence of the state exerts on its people. The political constitution is the expression of the people's moral and other aspirations, and is at the same time, in some large measure, the definition of their way of life. The political leadership is therefore burdened first of all with the duty to preserve intact its people's values and way of life. The leadership may therefore find itself in the logically embarrassing but practically justifiable position of one who must curtail freedom in order to preserve it for the future. An encroachment on democracy, for example, on the part of a democratic government is not a lie in itself, but becomes one when the vindication of it is insincere. The moral obligation of a government to be truthful is identically the same as that of an individual, in that there must be no doubt in the conscience of the leadership that the deviations in practice from the genuine ideals of the state are in the service of those ideals. It should go without saying that unqualified truthfulness and candor are more to be expected of individuals than of states, which have no greater power to appeal to for their safety than their own devices and must therefore include deception as well as force among their instruments. In fact, the argument may well be made that, when the state is compelled to choose between force and fraud, the latter is the less inhuman.

It might be contended that the moral law absolutely obliges states and individuals alike because the moral law has a divine origin. The reason might be granted and the conclusion nevertheless rejected because in any event God works his ways through the freedom of men, and to deny this is to impugn the omnipotence of God by suggesting that His will can be frustrated by the mere freedom of His creature. The inconclusiveness of an appeal to religion in this matter is indicated by the opposite conclusions reached by intense believers in the Middle East, where it can be demonstrated that some of the pious, of one or another religious faith, may be the most inflamed nationalists, while others may be hostile to the very idea of the national enterprise. The former might allow everything to the state power and the latter nothing, both alike and with equal reason claiming the support of revealed truth. Unless a civil authority that is immune to popular opinion is made the arbitrary interpreter of revelation, the divine basis of the absolute moral law will be determined according to the democratic principle, "vox populi vox dei," which implies the intolerable blasphemy that the meaning of the word of God might change every five years.

The question regarding relativist and "absolutist" moral standards seems to me to be capable of a reformulation that might make it more pertinent to situations known to exist, for example in the Middle East, where in Israel the tension is not between relative and fixed norms but rather between equally firmly valued principles of political life: democratic liberalism, survival of the state, and ancient moral teaching with all the sanction of divinity and custom recommending it. If the appeal to religion is problematic, if only because the appeal does not evoke an univocal response, perhaps the appeal to the democratic idea deserves to take precedence over the others as the ultimate ground of morals and politics. But there are states, and Israel is not the only one, where the absolutization of majority rule would, now or eventually, subvert the present regime. There is no known rule of morality, and if there were one it would be neglected, that calls upon a civil society knowingly and formally to destroy itself in the name of democracy or perhaps in the name of anything else. This omits the already mentioned clash between strict democracy and the

14

supremacy of religion. If there is an absolute moral criterion, democracy does not seem to supply it, although it might be argued that a democracy like that of Athens, in which the *demos* defined itself as by no means coextensive with the entire population, might seem to overcome some of the difficulties just mentioned.

Is survival the final and perhaps absolute ground of the public morality, and if so, is it different from the principle of private morality? This could be affirmed only at the cost of all considerations of humanity and decency, and least of all in any land where the works of Hitler and Stalin are remembered. I conclude that the only absolute ground of public morality is the vision, humanity, and unsentimental prudence of a leadership to which much is permitted that is forbidden to individuals because the power that supervenes over states, whether history, God or nature, unlike the power that rules within them, works in ways that only arrogant human beings claim to be privy to.

15

MORALITY AND ORDER IN THE PUBLIC DOMAIN

Gordon M. Freeman

The State of Israel is governing territories inhabited by a hostile population. The fundamental political questions in this situation must be addressed. What constitutes political legitimacy? What is the purpose of government? What are the limitations on the government's authority? When may governments utilize coercive force in order to gain compliance? All of these issues are included in the question posed by this symposium: Is there a difference between individual morality and the morality of public policy choices for a state or other political community?

The classic works of Jewish tradition have addressed these same issues. It will be the purpose here to examine the response from Jewish sources to these questions.,

It is clear that governments are authorized to use force in order to rule. Statements in Deuteronomy 17, I Samuel 8, Jeremiah 29:7 and Pirke Avot 3:2 substantiate that right under various conditions, including situations of apparent abuse and situations of questionable legitimacy. These statements understand that the primary concern of government is to maintain order. It may use coercive force in order to maintain order.

There is, then, a substantial difference between private morality and the morality of public policy. While the private person may defend himself against other private people who have no right to coerce him, government may use coercive force, and the citizen must obey, except for instances of abuse (which will be dealt with below). Governments are granted the right to use coercive force in order to gain compliance in the tasks of maintaining order and executing public policy. Individuals are not granted the right to use coercive force against others except in case of self-defense.

To illustrate this point, we may turn to the tax rebellions against David's government. These rebellions threatened the legitimacy of the government, and, in fact, after the death of Solomon, such a rebellion succeeded in creating the counter-government of Israel. David and Solomon used force to put down these

17

rebellions. And while the abuse of power was clearly challenged by the prophets (e.g., Nathan and Elijah), the use of force in putting down the tax rebellions was not challenged. It is clear that the government had the right to use coercive force to confront this challenge and maintain order.

Even in the case of the abuse of power against individuals, when the force of government was used in an immoral manner, the prophetic condemnation was against the abuse of that force and not against the use of force to maintain order.

It is important to note the farewell address of Samuel (I Samuel 12) and the plea of Moses before the Korach rebellion (Numbers 16:15). Both leaders go before the people, not apologizing for their use of coercive force in order to govern, but rather asking anyone if they had abused their power for personal gain. Both leaders understood that they had been authorized to rule for the public good.

There is a difference according to Jewish sources between public and private dimensions. In the former, coercive force is authorized in order to gain compliance. In the private sector such force is not authorized. The difference between the two is the difference between a gang of brigands and legitimate government.

One of the most dramatic examples of this difference is to be found in the statement in Avot 3:2. The Roman Empire, about which R. Hananiah is speaking, was rapacious and oppressive (see also Bereshit Rabbah 9:15). Its very legitimacy was questioned in Mishnah Nedarim 3:4, which stated that one could do almost anything to escape tax collectors sent by the Roman government. Yet the use of coercive force to maintain order was recognized even as a minimal duty of government. Later claims (during the Bar Kochba rebellion) against the Roman Empire were based on its attempt to outlaw the study of Torah, which was understood to be the very purpose of Jewish existence, not against its task to maintain order.

When a government is unable to maintain public order it loses its very legitimacy in the eyes of the governed. Unfortunately, in actual experience, unsheathed power often becomes abusive. There must be a clear differentiation between the morality of a specific policy and the manner by which that policy is executed. We have established the moral right of government to maintain order. But if it uses the pursuit of such a policy as a cover for abuse of power against individuals, the manner of execution must be condemned (the case of Elijah and Ahab). The very methods of maintaining order become an issue to be investigated.

The prophets contended that the moral basis of government must be the observance of the covenant. Manifestations of covenant observance were fighting idolatry and pursuing policies that were just and compassionate. While governments had to maintain order, their legitimacy had to have a moral foundation. Policy was examined in terms of these three issues: confronting idolatry as inimical to the exclusive covenant with God; maintaining justice; behaving in a compassionate manner. The latter is explained in terms of providing support and protection for the weak and vulnerable (widows, orphans, alien residents).

It is obvious that the prophetic tradition must be understood in the context of a less than perfect world, or else there would be no need to execute justice; compassion would have been ubiquitous.

Idolatry was the most important issue for the prophets; a government was measured by its ability to root out idolatrous practices. Idolatry was a covenantal matter: the state was constituted by the agreement between God and the people. The purpose of the people and all the institutions (including government) was to fulfill that exclusive agreement. Treason was defined in terms of straying from that agreement, or, in the words of the Bible, going astray after other gods. Manifestations of idolatry were to be found in a society lacking in justice and compassion.

During times of duress, can the task of maintaining public order override justice and compassion? That is, when the authority of the government is challenged through the use of force, may the government relax the pursuit of justice and compassion in the interest of maintaining public order? Or to state the question from another perspective, do those who challenge the very legitimacy of government in a violent manner thereby relinquish their rights to expect justice and compassion? If so, under what kind of conditions?

In the present political situation in Israel and the territories we are clearly dealing with a hostile population which does not recognize the legitimacy of the Israeli government. The issue of Israel's right to rule this population is beyond the scope of this paper. The fact of the matter is that it is governing this population. The reality is that it cannot relinquish its primary duty to maintain order until an alternative arrangement is found, whatever that might be. Either the population will recognize the legitimacy of the Israeli government (hardly likely under the present situation) or they will continue to refuse to recognize it. Compliance to the maintenance of order is yet another matter. Either a transference of the obligation to another governing entity will take place or not. But for the present, the Israeli government would be irresponsible if it did not use force to maintain order to protect all the inhabitants against violence.

Even though the Arab inhabitants of the territories might not recognize the legitimacy of Israeli authority, they do have the right to expect it to act with compassion and justice, as long as they accept responsibility to eschew violence, even while challenging the legitimacy of Israeli rule. More important, the population of Israel proper must demand that it act in this manner, or else the very moral basis of its governance would be legitimately questioned. However, under conditions of insurrection and rebellion, that is, the use of physical force to challenge the government, thereby challenging the right of the government to maintain order, the inhabitants have created a situation wherein compassion and justice toward individuals might be impossible to maintain. If those in rebellion have created a situation where the use of force will be necessary to maintain public order, they have also regarded manifestations of justice and compassion as indications of the inability of the government to maintain order or, alternatively, as attempts to demonstrate legitimacy which would be completely rejected.

Those who support the use of physical violence reject manifestations of justice and compassion since they would not recognize any act of the government to be acceptable. They must understand that such acts would be regarded as aggressive acts, methods of asserting legitimacy; hence, they would be rejected. However, those who do support the government must demand that while force might be required to maintain public order, that it be used judiciously, that it not be abused and that innocent persons not be victimized.

Once we accept the difference between the public and private domain and the means to test actions of government under a variety of conditions, absolutist vs. relativistic based positions on morality become spurious. It is clear that in the case of the territories the ability to govern is being challenged, i.e., if the Israeli government is unable to maintain order, it has no right to be there. It is an attempt to force perceived superior powers (e.g., the UN, the superpowers, etc.) to condemn the Israeli presence.

The paradox of this situation is abundantly clear. The government of Israel, in acquiring this territory, whether the means of acquisition is perceived as legitimate or not, has also acquired

20

the obligation to maintain order. This obligation is beyond any issues of policy; it is the foundation of government's very purpose. It might be that as a consequence of the rebellion, the government might be forced to leave that area, but it may not do so without an orderly transference of power to another entity which would have the task of maintaining public order. While the people of Israel and its government might chose a public policy in regard to the disposition of the territories, it may not give up its obligation to maintain order until another entity is established.

The dichotomy between expectations of Israelis on their government and expectations of those engaged in physical violence must also be explored. At first glance it does not seem to make sense that such a difference in perspectives would be possible. However, those who support the legitimacy of government must demand that in its execution of coercive force that abuse be avoided and justice and compassion be maintained. For those who have engaged in physical violence to have the same expectation is clearly ridiculous, for even acts of justice and compassion would be interpreted as a means to support the claims of the government which they have rejected.

The very basis of making moral judgements in the case of the territories must be examined in the light of the primary prophetic demand of maintaining the covenant: the warning against idolatry. Idolatry must be explained today in terms of creating images and attributing power to those images which then direct the actions of those who support them. People create images with the illusion that they have control in a dangerous and dynamic world. Furthermore, in the pursuit of idolatry, the images created by each individual destroy the shared agreement that establishes the society. If each has a right to create and be governed by his own image, then each has created his own reality that, while it might be a source of solace and comfort, will eventually be destructive of that society.

Those images are most often illusions of wishful thinking, projecting what we would like the world to be rather than confronting reality with all of its implacable problems. Those individual-based images make the pursuit of consensus impossible.

These days, images are created for us through the use of technology. It is almost impossible to determine what is real and what is not. What images are created and what public policy are those images supporting? Moral positions not based on reality are the most dangerous. The prophets warned that the pursuit of images rather than confronting reality will lead to disastrous public policy decisions (e.g., Jeremiah on peace).

The purpose of government is to govern. If the government is chosen by the people, it obviously has the right to govern it. If it conquers a territory and is unable to incorporate that territory, does it have the right to rule over it? What right does any government have to govern conquered and unincorporated territory, the inhabitants of which do not recognize its very legitimacy? Whereas various political interests in Israel may have claimed legitimate rights of governance by virtue of conquest and/or history, the government of Israel has not done so. It has not incorporated or annexed the West Bank or Gaza. Rather, it has stated that the disposition of the territories is to be determined through the process of negotiation with those parties which recognize the legitimacy of the State of Israel. Until that time comes, the government of Israel is obligated to maintain public order even in those areas of contention, abiding by its moral covenant to rule with justice and compassion undetered by illusionary solutions to real problems.

MORALITY AND PUBLIC POLICY IN THE CURRENT ISRAEL-ARAB CONFRONTATION

Murray Friedman

Speaking quite personally, I see no special distinction between the code of morality that should guide an individual and the well-being of the state.

The first rule of life as we confront it on a practical level is to protect those near and dear to us whether they be one's family or the larger families in which we live. The political community is, of course, an example of the latter. For a people who have such a bloody history as the Jews, and the State of Israel surrounded as it is by neighbors bent on her destruction if they had but the power or the influence to accomplish this, security has to be the primary consideration.

That Israel and through it the Jewish people have the strength to defend themselves is one of the extraordinary events in modern Jewish history. Powerlessness throughout much of that history has been the greatest form of Jewish immorality. The weak have no ability to defend themselves. They have to depend, as Blanche DuBois said in Tennessee Williams' *A Streetcar Named Desire*, on "the kindness of strangers." One remembers the days when non-Jewish friends would wring their hands about "the poor Jews" but could not or would not do much to help. I would rather that Jews had the strength to defend themselves, with all the problems this sometimes entails, than enjoy the pity of others.

It is more than disturbing to watch critics of Israel's behavior on the West Bank and Gaza condemning its hard-line tactics in dealing with the uprisings there and pressing the Jewish state to take major risks for peace. As I write this, the PLO has just met in Algiers and issued a proclamation hinting at its recognition of Israel. As one reads the fine print, we discover that such "recognition" is highly ambiguous. It seeks to cut out Jerusalem from the Jewish state and does not renounce violence within its borders. Still it is being hailed by those on the political Left and even some moderates as a good first step. Some "first step"!

It is of course true that Judaism or at least Jewishness requires

23

Jews to adhere to broader, civilizing goals than self-interest. But I have come to resent in recent years the view, maintained by many, that Israel must be held not only to higher values than other nations but often to unrealizable objectives. It bothers me deeply, for example, that groups like the American Friends Service Committee, the New Jewish Agenda, and the Left generally focus so heavily on Israel's small amount of trade with South Africa. Why is there so little condemnation of African and Arab as well as Western nations that engage in far greater amounts of trade? There is involved here not only a large dose of hypocrisy but a more fundamental animus that has to be watched in the light of Jewish historical experience. In the circumstances in which Israel finds itself today, and as nations go, I believe it has done comparatively well in living up to its democratic traditions.

The issue of how to protect oneself once one has sufficient strength to do so is, of course, complicated. As an American Jew who has chosen not to live out his life in Israel, I have always hesitated to give advice to that state on matters involving security. Those who have to pay in blood the price of any miscalculation must have the last word here even if American Jews can and should discuss their views on such a serious subject with Israeli authorities.

But since the questions posed here have to be answered, had I been an Israeli, I probably would have voted for Shimon Peres in the recent election. I would have done so because of his willingness to test the waters of any possible changes in the usual Arab countries' intransigence as well as their ambiguous statements emanating out of Algiers. That kind of relativistic position I would be prepared to go along with.

But in my heart of hearts I sense that Prime Minister Yitzhak Shamir and Likud are probably the only forces capable of making peace with the Arabs. It has been the recent experience we have had of Begin with Egypt and Reagan on nuclear disarmament with the Soviet Union that those who truly seek peace and operate from a position of strength practice, ultimately, the "higher morality." For peace as I see it is not best accomplished by softening the hearts of antagonists and utopian dreams but by a practical recognition of the realities of power. When the Arabs come to the peace table and deal with Israel directly, then the possibility of making peace, at least in this part of the Middle East, and morality have the breathing space they need to exist. In the meantime, it is well to keep one's powder dry.

PUBLIC HUMANISM, AN EXERCISE IN SELF-DESTRUCTION

Manfred Gerstenfeld

"Don't believe a word if you hear the younger generation talk about the new morality."
— Jose Ortega Y Gasset, *La rebelion de las masas* (1930)[1]

A Highly Imperfect World

If the Palestinians were under Iraqi rule and rebelled in the *intifada* way many of them would be dead by now. The Western world and media would not care much about them or whether the Iraqis were right or wrong in killing them. The same is true for the great majority of church leaders, humanists, socialists, assorted leftists and/or progressives.

The media like easy and riskless access to the dead. Corpses to be viewed should preferably be from countries with good communications. Journalists prefer places with relatively low risk for their lives to those where they may be harmed if they do not exercise self-censure. From a pragmatic point of view this makes sense. They are in the communications business and not in heroism.

An additional incentive for media to view the dead is if they are located in a democratic country and if the hotels where one sojourns are relatively comfortable and near the place of action. The American Colony Hotel in Jerusalem, close to *intifada* land, is such a location, even if corpses in much greater quantities can be discovered elsewhere in the world.

As far as Western governments are concerned, business potential is an excellent consideration to overlook chemical warfare or, if it cannot be overlooked entirely, to belittle it. What has been written here so far may be a bit schematic. That does not make it untrue. If one were to claim the opposite of most of the preceding statements, their lie content would increase substantially.

Morality expresses itself largely through self-restraint. "When your enemy falls you shall not rejoice."[2] This biblical quotation demonstrates well how Judaism views morality. It makes the major demand on man to restrain himself. It does not request him to do the unnatural and cry about the falling of the enemy. Judaism is not a religion which nominally propagates turning the other cheek. It is a religion of: "If somebody comes to kill you, get up early to kill him."[3] But next to the number of dead the religion of the cheekturners has produced over the ages, the *intifada* pales into marginality.

Such a comparison has to be made reluctantly as the dying of people should not be considered insignificant. However, without comparisons there are no norms and standards of behavior. Thus when one assesses morality, concrete situations have to be examined. How did and do individuals and communities perform under duress? How much damage did they do? How does this compare with others under somewhat similar circumstances? As a result thereof, was their behavior relatively moral or immoral?

Decisions and Consequences

The private individual in a democratic state has more control over his life than in any other system of government. He has potentially many choices to determine how he lives. If he wishes so, he can devote his life to the poor, give to charity whatever he owns, and love his neighbor more than himself even if that neighbor is despicable.

Ideally a free man makes his own decisions, with the related risks and rewards, and carries the consequences thereof. In retrospect, the irresponsible decision of the late Swedish Prime Minister Olaf Palme to send his bodyguards away demonstrates this in the extreme. When he was shot thereafter, he paid with his life for his erroneous judgment. Nobody else was endangered. It is very rare in real life that such a clear relation can be established between a politician's act and its consequences.

The citizen who behaves very charitably may pay the price for his convictions and become a victim of his good deeds. This can be exceptionally moral, noble and admirable if one sacrifices or risks one's life to save somebody else's. However, the problem becomes one for society if other citizens or the community have to pay part of the price.

Almost 500 years ago the following was written: "The gulf between how one should live and how one does live is so wide that a man who neglects what is actually done for what should be done learns the way to self-destruction rather than self-preservation. The fact is that a man who wants to act virtuously necessarily comes to grief among so many who are not virtuous."[4]

Machiavelli, the author of the previous sentences, was despised by both ruling politicians and humanists up to our own days. This does not mean that his analysis was incorrect, rather the contrary. What was worse, he said the truth in a clear and concise way.

Regional Ethics and Challenges

In public behavior, morality can only be a dominant force in noncritical situations. Nations should not take undue risks. Their life expectancy, unlike that of human beings, is not limited by physical constraints. Mysticism cannot and should not dominate public policy. Neither should morality on fateful issues even though it is a factor to be taken into consideration. Governments should not be charitable in their major decisions. If they are fair that is already quite remarkable. When a crucial challenge to a nation arises it has to be met. The morality of a nation expresses itself in the way it uses its tools in confrontation with an enemy.

President Carter's pseudohumanism in helping to demote the Shah of Iran caused much damage to the Iranian people. A cruel system was replaced by an infinitely more cruel one. The United States was subsequently humiliated by the occupation of its embassy in Teheran and the failure of its rescue attempt. Partly as a result thereof, Carter failed to get reelected in 1980. Thus, even in complex situations, it can occasionally be demonstrated that a politician has to pay for his mistakes.

The PLO for a long time behaved inside Israel without self-restraint. It did as much damage as it could. If it had achieved what it wanted it would have destroyed the State of Israel and killed the Jews or driven them out. Most states in the world claim that the PLO is the representative organization of the Palestinians. Moral considerations facing such an enemy must be of a totally different nature than those of a country facing enemies with which it has a minor border dispute. Western regional ethics and values in the face of such a Middle Eastern regional challenge are inadequate at best.

When Egypt made peace with Israel it was not because it had

come to the insight that its past attempts to destroy Israel had been morally wrong. Peace, which should have been the first approach, is for the Arabs the ultimate one, when all forceful approaches have failed. Recently the PLO also has started to make somewhat different noises about Israel. These are not an indication of its advancing humanism but rather of the failure of all its other alternatives.

The Perversity of Absolute Morality

Absolutely moral nations do not exist. They would have been wiped out before they came into being. Absolute morality is perverse because it leads to the destruction of the moral rather than the immoral. The world is not only less than perfect but highly imperfect. This strengthens the argument that self-restraint shown by a nation should be viewed in comparison with the behavior of other nations under as comparable as possible circumstances.

It is unreasonable to compare Israel's actual behavior with that of Britain, France or the United States of today. Most "civilized, humane" Western nations have so much bloodshed in their past that they prefer to be judged on the basis of their most recent present. They state that conditions have evolved since they violently suppressed others. The present untested generation criticizes its predecessors and claims that it would have reacted differently, more humanely, under the same circumstances. Judaism has shown more judgment than the so-called progressives of the Western world in Hillel's saying: "Do not judge your fellow man until you are in his place."[5]

Technology has given the major impetus through which humanity has evolved over the ages. Changes in humanitarian attitudes are not due to the greater insight of the later generations compared to earlier ones. They are largely a function of technology, both for good and for ill. The twentieth century is a more criminal one than most, if not all, previous ones. Technology made crime possible at a much larger scale than before. Atilla the Hun killed fewer people than Hitler not because he was of a gentler inclination, but because he lacked the technology to murder on an industrial scale.

Technology has made democracy beyond the city-state a viable form of government. It has created the relative prosperity which stable noncorrupt democracies require. It also has made possible the necessary diffusion of knowledge on a large scale. Democracy is a luxury of modern society, which relatively few nations allow themselves.

The humanitarian attitude of Western democracies, though, is largely a function of the benign conditions under which they live. If they were to come under duress they would have to abolish certain democratic rights as some of the harder pressed nations did during the Second World War. The temporary spirit of our time is such that it promotes a great variety of "progressive" fallacies as far as the character of human nature is concerned.

One of the most surprising phenomena in Israel's short history is its ability to survive relatively well as a democracy, this in spite of the duress under which it lives and the undemocratic character of the nations which surround it. While Israel has to limit certain democratic rights, it scores remarkably well if one takes into account, as one should do, the fact that all neighboring nations were committed to its destruction for most of its history.

The main purpose of the State of Israel is to be a national home for the Jewish people which has been so heavily persecuted for such a long time. Survival of this state, preferably as a democracy, should be its prime target. It becomes more and more doubtful whether the two peoples, Jews and Arabs, in rather similar numbers, can coexist within one state framework.

In this context peace, which by necessity means a division of the British Mandate territory between Jews and Arabs, is by far the preferred solution out of today's labile situation. The "non-peace" status quo cannot last for many more decades and must lead to the massive expulsion of either Palestinian Arabs or Jews.

Morality and self-restraint are necessary ingredients in Israel's decision-making. How much of these are applied is not an absolute issue but depends on the circumstances. Israel has never claimed that all is permitted against its enemies; still it may well have to take tougher actions against them in the future if no peace agreement is reached.

As said before, any comparison of behavior of nations under duress has to be made on the basis of defined criteria. Quantitative analysis also has to be carried out. Thus let us select a few cases out of the history and present of Western nations which arrogantly reproach Israel for its behavior.

The Noble British Nation

The United Kingdom is very suitable for comparison with Israel because it was the Mandatory power in Palestine and has operated in the same geographical environment. At the time of the pre-Second World War Arab uprising in Palestine (1936-1939), the British occasionally shot Arabs at random in villages from which terrorists came. In the Israeli television series *Pillar of Fire*, an Arab eyewitness was interviewed about how the British suppressed the uprising once they had identified which villages supported the rebels:

> The British commander arrived...and entered the village of Matsar. He told the villagers: "I shall shoot a few of you, or you tell me who shot." Of course the people did not tell him....He said: "You have ten minutes." After ten minutes he said: "You have five more minutes." The five minutes passed. He then said: "Stand in a row," and counted — 1, 2, 3, 4 until 9. He caught the tenth and killed him. He counted again to 9, caught the tenth and killed him. This way he killed three people. He left them and went away.[6]

In the Second World War the British bombed the city of Dresden when there was already little doubt as to the outcome of the war. Many tens of thousands of civilians were killed. As the Germans had heavily bombed British cities before, nobody contested the morality or necessity of the bombing in Britain at the time it happened.

One cannot prove that the British government of today would do the same after being under similar duress. Parts of British public opinion nowadays consider the Dresden bombing superfluous. This is fairly meaningless because it means morally judging a totally different historical situation in the U.K.'s rather relaxed situation of today.

Nevertheless, since Britain is fighting terrorists today in Northern Ireland, a glimpse can be obtained of how the British act under slight duress. The IRA does not endanger the United Kingdom's existence. It does not want to establish another state on the British mainland. It contests British rule in a relatively minor area.

Time magazine claims: "The debate over shoot-to-kill is underscored by one salient fact: in the course of operations against the IRA, the SAS has never been known to take a prisoner."[7] When the SAS security services shot three unarmed members of the IRA in Gibraltar in March 1988, their action was investigated by a magistrate. The appointed jury came to the verdict that the action had been "lawful killing."

Britain also provides other examples of Western hypocrisy. It favors self-determination for the Palestinians. It intends, however, to hand over Hongkong later this century to China, a country where virtually no democratic rights are respected, this without asking its inhabitants whether they want it.

"Britain has become an insecure society, not at peace with itself, with increasing stress, family break-up, poverty, crime, drug and alcohol abuse and a terrifying spread of violence from football terraces to quiet towns."[8] This is a statement by Neil Kinnock, the leader of Labour, Britain's second largest party. It is not exactly clear on what basis the British minister Mellor was critical of Israel when he came to Israel at the beginning of the *intifada*. Perhaps next time when an Israeli minister visits the U.K. he should ask that a visit to a typical U.K. slum area be included in his program. A few scathing comments on Northern Ireland and the U.K.'s policy there might make the balance more even.

France, America and Others

An additional useful criterion in analyzing a country's behavior is whether and in what circumstances death sentences are carried out. France, which applies this penalty, is another nation full of self-appointed judges of other people's behavior. Since the Second World War it has acted with extreme cruelty in both Indochina and Algeria, even though the loss of these territories did not endanger the survival of France.

One interesting French death sentence may be taken as an example. In August 1962 at Petit Clamart outside Paris, an attempt was made on the life of then-President of France Charles de Gaulle. The general escaped unharmed, still Bastien Thiry, one of those making the attempt, was condemned to death and executed.

Israel has not hanged its own traitors. It has not carried out a death sentence against any Arab terrorist even if he murdered women and children who did not provoke him. The soft Israeli attitude may well be a mistake, in particular after one of the terrorist chiefs, Jibril, managed in a prisoner exchange to free many of his people.

Western moralists pretend that governments can always, under all circumstances, control their soldiers. France has recently been facing some problems in its Pacific territory of New Caledonia, which most Frenchmen cannot locate on a map within a thousand kilometers of accuracy. The number of incidents there was small by *intifada* standards. However, when French soldiers captured rebels they killed a few of those taken prisoner.

After Pearl Harbor, the Americans interned their citizens of Japanese origin without any proof of hostile behavior. Then the United States recruited some of them to fight in bloody battles to prove their loyalty to the United States. Today, part of American public opinion regrets that action, but that is at best secondary. Primary is how America behaved in the given situation.

Some attention should also be given to the Spanish Civil War because it is such a beloved leftist cause. The crimes committed by both sides were barbaric to an extent few people outside Spain realize. As far as the "good side," i.e., Republican Spain, is concerned, the following quotation from one of the leading foreign historians on the subject is illuminating: "The Nationalists since the War have named a figure of 85,940 for all reputed murdered or executed in Republican Spain during the war. This calculation is certainly not an underestimation, though it compares favorably with the wilder accusations of three or four hundred thousand made during the course of the war."[9]

A large part of the Jewish population of Israel has great doubts about the loyalty of many Israeli Arabs towards the state. There are sufficient indications that these suspicions are justified. After PLO leader Abu Jihad was killed, a mourning meeting was held by Arab students at Hebrew University. The extreme liberalism of the university authorities who permitted this gathering enables one to get a good insight into the loyalties of some Israeli Arabs. Nevertheless, Israel has not recruited Arab university students and forced them to suppress the *intifada* as a sign of their loyalty to the state.

In the duress of its situation, Israel has not resorted to the British, French or American methods of massive indiscriminate bombing of civilians, executing or hanging terrorists or traitors, and sending Arab citizens into battle to die to prove their loyalty to the state. This may well be a luxurious attitude towards life.

Israel's citizens and its enemies can only be glad that so far it can afford these luxuries and that it is willing to show greater self-restraint than the "humane" Western nations.

The Lucky Nations

Some nations have more luck than others. Sweden has not had a war for a long time. This is not a sign of the smartness of its government or people. Denmark or the Netherlands would also gladly have stayed out of the Second World War, but did not have the choice, as Hitler attacked them. If one sees how clumsily Sweden has behaved in the investigation of the Palme murder and how its defense system seems to be riddled with highly placed traitors, one wonders whether this nation could have survived under a fraction of the duress Israel has withstood since it came into being.

The Dutch are a less lucky nation than the Swedes because they were attacked by the Germans and suffered a severe occupation. In 1940 the ill-prepared Dutch army collapsed rapidly. Luck is a relative matter also on the downside. The fate of the Dutch non-Jews under German occupation compared very favorably with that of the Dutch Jews. While the non-Jews suffered, 80 percent of the Jews were annihilated.

The Dutch were unable to free themselves from the Germans and had to be freed by their allies. Israel has to fight for its own freedom. Perhaps Dutch politicians should be more careful when criticizing Israel. A nation which could not protect or free itself has no right to criticize other nations. Also Dutch colonial history in this and the previous century contains an amount of cruelty and betrayal one would not have expected from a nation with such a humane image.

If Hafez el Assad Followed Buber

A critical consideration in the amount of self-restraint shown is against whom one fights. Gentlemen fighting among each other behave differently from street-fighters. Israel's Arab neighbors are rather cruel nations. In Black September, thousands of Palestinians were killed at the order of the well-educated Hashemite King Hussein who is so liked by the media. He would have handled the *intifada* more effectively and in shorter time, not necessarily with fewer dead. The Algerian government of President Chadli Benjedid has demonstrated once again that there are alternatives to Israel's way of suppressing disorders. A few hundred people were killed in less than a week in October 1988.

Syrian President Hafez el Assad is one of those rulers who has given ample proof of how Arab rulers can behave. In February 1982 he suppressed the Muslim Brotherhood riots in Hamat with an estimated 30,000 civilian dead. It was a pity for those Syrians killed that Assad was not an adherent of Martin Buber. Then he might have asked himself whether he could not have achieved his aims by killing "only" 27,000 or 24,000.

Iraq in its war against Iran has made chemical warfare reemerge. Like Iran it has bombed civilian targets without discrimination. The limitations in this war were not prescribed by moral self-restraint, but only by technological limitations and fear of retaliation. Iraq's suppression of the Kurds does not elicit many Western government declarations regarding the right to self-determination of the latter.

Those who do not practice self-restraint and operate on the basis of maximum ability to harm their enemies do not have to sustain moral discussions. In a democracy under duress, every action has to be analyzed. That is what democracy is about and continuously marginal decisions have to be made. Where is one going too far under the circumstances and where not? In a multi-origin society such as Israel norms are even more difficult to set. Thus the issues have to be debated at length, even if those discussions also serve the pathological enemies of Israel. These by now include not only the traditional anti-Semites of the right, but also many leftists.

Do Humanists Merit a State?

In the Lebanese war much attention was given to the murders at Sabra and Shatila. Arabs murdered Arabs as had happened so often in Lebanon before and since. In this case (and this too was nothing exceptional) the murderers were Christians. That did not cause any major distress to their humanist coreligionists in the Western world. Israel's involvement, however, was investigated in Israel by a public inquiry commission. The Israeli aspect of the issue, whatever its importance, was secondary. Yet it has become the only one to stick in the mind.

Was it Israel's strength or its weakness to investigate its role in the Sabra and Shatila murders in such a major way? Only time will tell. No nation can loosen itself from its past, particularly not a nation with a long history and which sees its history as a continuous process. Israel cannot rapidly shake diaspora thinking out of its system, even if some of its concepts, both paranoiac and humanistic, are harmful in a Jewish state.

The Jews lived in the diaspora for a long time as a nonviolent minority and developed a totally unrealistic view of how a nation should defend itself. Overstressing conscientious aspects by definition betrays lack of judgment on critical public issues of a state. The Jews in biblical times who left Egypt were unable to enter the Promised Land because of their inability to rid themselves rapidly of their slave mentality. Many of the progressive Jews abroad today have a humanistic mentality, which if practiced by Israel would lead to its destruction. Abuse of religious terminology such as "the Chosen People" and "to be a light to the nations" only confuses the subject.

Nations which have too much compassion and understanding for their mortal enemies may not merit a state. If the biblical Jews had a bleeding heart mentality in their encounters with Amalek, Jericho and Ai, there would not have been a Jewish nation or a State of Israel. Neither would Jews have lived, which means no Christianity, no Crusades, no Inquisition. The world might still have been an interesting place to live. Western society would have had to limp along on its Greek-Roman heritage without the Judeo-Christian one. Without Christianity its history might perhaps have been less cruel.

Courseware on Fascistoid Journalists

For those in power in politics, business, media or anywhere else, hypocrisy is a much more common characteristic than morality. The last decade with its communications explosion has made the visual media emerge as major pseudomoral judges of behavior. One cannot neglect the effect the media are having on Israel's image abroad and this is a problem it has to come to grips with.

If one compares the reporting on the Seoul Olympics of many

Western television stations with that on the *intifada*, their hypocrisy can be well-illustrated. While the reporting on the sports event was panoramic and full, that of the disorders was biased and selective. If one were to assemble the aggregated Israel reporting of some of the major television stations during the past year, one would have excellent material to teach a course on fascistoid journalists in a democratic society.

One would have expected that as far as international conflicts in the world are concerned, the main attention of the Western media would go to the most violent ones, those with the largest numbers of killed and maimed per unit of time and those where the most cruel killing methods were used. Violent conflicts are real ones and should be subject to more professionalism in reporting than sports which are competitive games. Compared to 1988 killings in Iran, Iraq, Afghanistan and Burundi, the *intifada* merits a minor mention only.

A very telling example of how oriented selectiveness of news falsifies the truth was provided by Italy's largest circulation daily, *La Repubblica*. On October 19, 1988, after ten months of *intifada*, it carried on its front page a picture of a Palestinian Arab child shot dead, with the comments: "Five-year-old Palestinian killed in Ciajordan," "The Israelis shoot, also a 14-year-old boy killed" and "The small Diah Jihad Mohamed, killed at Nablus while he played in the school courtyard." These were the only front page comments on this issue. For the background on this news item one had to look at one of the inner pages of the paper.

The dead boy was the front page photographic event of the day among the five billion people who populate the world. By comparison, the previous day, October 19th, *La Repubblica* carried at the same spot on the front page a picture of a plane crash near Rome in which over 30 people died. The next day, October 20th, it published there a picture from a collision of two planes in India with over 160 dead.

La Repubblica also publishes a booklet every year with the main events of the year and its key articles. In the 1982 edition the disorders in the Syrian town of Hamat and its 30,000 civilian dead are not even mentioned.

Part of the blame for the *intifada* image also falls on the Israeli government. It should have known how the media function and not have given television the occasion to film in Judea and Samaria. Governments of democracies under duress should not play into the hands of their enemies. The "balance of rights" is a more sensible approach to democracy than the media-promoted "right to know."

Justified attention has been given to the danger to Israel's democratic character of the extreme rightist Kach party. The Jewish self-haters, masochists and flagellants on the other side of the political spectrum have by now become a similar problem. Still Israel has shown an almost incredible strength as a participatory democracy. In the Knesset elections of November 1988 about 80 percent of the population voted, as against about 50 percent in the American presidential election and about a third in the French referendum about the future of New Caledonia, which took place at around the same time.

The Arabs have carried out an infamous propaganda campaign against Israel for a long time and have been somewhat successful. Today Westerners too occasionally speak about "Israeli Nazi methods." The time may well have come for Israel to finally start to hit back.

Israel, the Jew of the Nations

The issue under discussion is so complex that it can perhaps best be concluded in the form of questions. Were the British immoral when they bombed Dresden, the Americans when they dropped the atom bombs on Hiroshima and Nagasaki, the Czechs when they drove the Sudeten Germans out? If they were not immoral, then Israel has so far been almost a "holy country" in dealing with the *intifada*. On the other hand, if every country in its public policy is immoral, why should Israel be the only moral nation in the world and run risks for the cause of morality which nobody else is willing to take.

The problem of the public morality of Israel is a largely artificial one. By any criteria Israel has performed well. All nations have their sadists. The humanists base themselves on the fallacy that man is intrinsically good. In reality, the Gauss curve of real life applies to Israeli policemen or soldiers as well as everyone else.

Some nations like the British, not having significant wars at hand, kill or mutilate for football, others when in uniform. It is doubtful whether the British football hooligans would have made very humane soldiers in a war, keen to respect civil rights. As Israel is a state which faces a large number of incidents, some soldiers will act sadistically. The more incidents, the more sadism. It is unavoidable and the best one can do is to investigate as much as one can and to punish the major excesses.

In the ultimate factual analysis it is the numbers which count. Emotions are part of the checks and balances of the human system. In responsible public policy emotions have only a minor role to play. The United States, in one mistake, shot down an Iranian civilian plane with more dead than the *intifada* during more than nine months. Perhaps the Americans should have shown some self-restraint at the risk of being the victims rather than the attackers. They did not and that is what counts.

The Jews have been so heavily persecuted in the past that they carry out continuous soul-searching and are comparatively reluctant to do harm to others. Masochism is often confused with morality. If some American humanistic Jews want to beat themselves to pulp over Israel's actions in their Yom Kippur prayers, that is their problem. It would have been better though if they had come to Israel to participate in the building of the country. But once they start to make systematic negative comments in public about Israel, their self-hate should be exposed.

Those Western nations which have committed such heavy bloodshed in the past will do the same again in the future when the need arises and also sometimes when it is not necessary. Israel's problem in the Western world is not its morality, which so far can stand up to any comparison. The real problem is its being out of phase with the present mood of pseudohumanist thinking of large parts of the Western population. This mood will change when new challenges emerge.

States have to struggle on. Some nations live under much more duress than others. Israel finds itself in an exceptional position. Anti-Semitism reflected a totally out of proportion attitude towards the Jewish minority. The small State of Israel has become the Jew of the nations. Morality in Israel's public policy has become part of a universal issue which can only become more complex with the passing of time.

Notes

1.   Jose Ortega Y Gasset. "Der Aufstand der Massen." Rowohlt, p. 139, (translated from German).

2.   Proverbs 24:17.

3.   Rashi's commentary on Exodus 22:1.

4.   Niccolo Machiavelli. *The Prince*. Penguin Classics, p. 91.

5.   Pirke Avoth 2:5.

6.   Interview with Muhmad Zuabi. *Piller of Fire*. Keter-Shikmona, p. 243 (Hebrew).

7.   "Deadly games. Britain's army and the IRA play tit for tat," *Time* (September 19, 1988).

8.   Neil Kinnock at the Labour Conference in Blackpool, October 4, 1988. As quoted in *The Guardian* (October 5, 1988).

9.   Hugh Thomas. *The Spanish Civil War*. Harper and Row, 1963, p. 173.

POLITICS AND THE ETHICS OF JUDAISM

Robert Gordis

Jews the world over in Israel and in the diaspora are deeply disturbed not only by the ongoing bloodshed caused by the Arab resistance, but even more by the violence that the state has felt compelled to use against the *intifada*. As men and women of moral sensitivity, they are conscious of the discrepancy between the ethical ideals they regard as binding in their personal lives, and the "less than perfect" measures that have been employed by the Israeli government to suppress the Arab uprising.

Our present concern is not to argue the merits or defects of various approaches to this difficult problem, but rather to discuss a perennial issue of which the present situation in Israel has made us painfully aware, the old question debated by moral philosophers, statesmen and people of good will, the relationship of morality to public policy in general and to international affairs in particular.

Historically, there have been three major approaches to the problem of the relevance of ethical standards to the foreign policy of nations. The oldest view, the most widely practiced and the least often articulated, maintains that there is no connection between ethical standards and international affairs. For this school of thought, foreign policy is exclusively an instrument for advancing the interests of the state, whose leaders are obligated to use all the means at their disposal, with no concern for moral considerations. The classic expression of this viewpoint is to be found in Machiavelli's *The Prince*, which seeks to train the ruler to manipulate public affairs in accordance with the practical needs of the hour. Centuries later, Karl Marx, who defined religion as the opiate of the people, together with his associate, Friedrich Engels, sought to buttress the view that ethical standards are the instrument by which religion attempts to enforce obedience to the status quo upon the oppressed groups in society. It therefore follows that ethical considerations are merely a facade or a tool, possessing no genuine validity of their own. In our century, totalitarian dictatorships, Fascist, Nazi and Communist, have not hesitated to employ such terms as "democracy," "freedom," and "peace" in their vocabulary as conscious disguises for achieving non-moral ends. And if a philosophy of ethics is desiderated, "the good" is defined in a dictatorship, whatever its hue — black, brown or red — as whatever advances the interest of the state, the race, or the party. In democratic lands, those who adopt this view of our problem remind us first that politics is the art of the possible, and second, that in our grossly imperfect world, the possible is always less than good.

At the opposite pole from this cynical approach is an attitude which has relatively few advocates today — the position of the idealist. There is a current tendency which must be guarded against, to over-simplify the position and exaggerate its naivete. Yet it remains true that fundamentally this attitude derived from a strong optimism with regard to human nature and its capacities and, as a corollary, from the belief in virtually automatic progress in history, moving inevitably toward greater justice and peace in international affairs.

The ideological sources of the liberal faith are to be found in eighteenth century secular humanism, expressed, for example, in Rousseau's faith in the fundamental goodness of man, which has been corrupted by the artificialities of civilization, and in Condorcet's doctrine of the perfectibility of human nature. A figure as distant from the philosophers of the Age of Reason as Hegel declared that *Weltgeschichte ist Weltgericht*. When the Kingdom of God was interpreted in purely secular terms, the congruence of the rational humanism of the eighteenth century and the religious idealism of the Scriptures seemed complete.

The idealism of the political liberal, whether derived from secular or from religious sources, suffered major setbacks in the mid-twentieth century. The "war to end war" and "make the world safe for democracy" succeeded in neither objective. The Second World War marked a desperate attempt by the free nations to destroy the manifestations of bestiality deeply rooted in human nature.

The Fascist and Nazi varieties of totalitarianism were overthrown, but their features were absorbed into the various dictatorships and military regimes in Africa, Asia and Latin America.

The problems of the present are compounded by memories of the past and fears for the future. Confronted by the mass of misery and cruelty visited upon the human race in two world wars which reached the nadir of degradation in the unspeakable horror of the Holocaust, and confronted by the unimaginable terrors of nuclear catastrophe, many former idealists relapsed into cynical disillusion.

Another alternative, by all odds the most popular, has, however, found a wide response — that of the "realists" in politics. Many of them are religious believers and find in the Bible the source of their conception of human nature. They declare that man's weaknesses are the basic constituents of his nature, so that all his activities are at worst evil and at best morally ambiguous. Since the vices of pride, self-assertion, and the will to power inevitably find expression in the area of political activity, politics cannot be reasonably expected to obey the dictates of ethics — the best that can be hoped for is the choices of the least evil of alternatives. Any effort to invoke moral principles in politics must lead to defeat, if not to disaster, because the nature of reality does not conform to the demands of the ethical conscience. This widespread school of thought would unhesitatingly answer in the affirmative their question — is there a basic difference between individual morality and the morality of public policy choices for a political community.

I would suggest that all three answers rest upon several prior assumptions that are by no means self-evident or true.

Conceivably, moral philosophers in an ivory tower and religious leaders communing with their God could arrive at a set of universal principles acceptable to all human beings. This has, indeed, been the case with Hillel's Golden Rule and Kant's Categorical Imperative, but in the work-a-day in which men and nations live and function and struggle, confronted by concrete situations they are motivated and guided not by a single, universal doctrine, but by particular — and particularistic — systems of ethics which derive from their own personal background and group experience.

The two great religious traditions in the West, Judaism and Christianity, share much in common. They both revere the same Scripture and sacred history. Since Christianity arose within the Jewish community and its earliest and most influential figures were Jews, they have had an association, not always happy, for twenty centuries. Hence there is an element of validity in the term, "the Judeo-Christian tradition," which has won wide acceptance in the West, particularly in the United States. But it has had the unfortunate effect of obscuring fundamental differences between the two "partners" that are scarcely less significant than the similarities. One of the most important divergences is the profound contrast in their respective conceptions of human nature and consequently in the system of morality that each tradition has fashioned.

I submit that *only if the Christian view of human nature and its ethical code is accepted are we confronted by the difference "between individual morality and public policy."*

For its view of human nature, classical Christianity takes as its point of departure the doctrine of "original sin," the belief that the sin of Adam and Eve in the Garden of Eden placed an ineradicable taint upon the human race and stamped human nature as essentially evil, redeemable only by faith in the "righteous Teacher" of the Qumran scrolls or Jesus or another savior.

This essentially negative view of human nature was a reflex of the pessimism that gripped wide sections of Greco-Roman society, as classical paganism disintegrated in the first centuries of the Common Era. Among the Jews in Palestine, where the faith in a just God beat powerfully, the Roman oppression bred a passionate belief that a cataclysm that would usher in the kingdom of God was imminent. Since the structures of society were on the threshold of annihilation, only the individual mattered.

The interim ethic of self abnegation expresses itself in terms of emotional attitudes, extolling virtues like love and charity, rather than in the promulgation of specific norms of conduct through a system of law. In fact, the New Testament tends to decry such efforts as legalism as an impersonal and heartless approach to the problems of human relationships. Its antinomian bias, as Paul indicates, is directed not merely against the ritual elements of the law, but against ethical enactments as well: "The letter kills, but the spirit gives life" (Corinthians 3:6).

The ethics of self-abnegation have also been the source of the doctrine of non-resistance to evil. It may, incidentally, be pointed out — a fact little known — that the New Testament teaching of "turning the other cheek" (Matthew 5:39) is derived from the Hebrew Bible: "It is good for a man to bear the yoke in his youth, to put his mouth in the dust; there may yet be hope that in giving his cheek to smiters, let him be surfeited with insults" (Lamentations 3:17-20). In the Hebrew Bible, however, this behavior is described as a tragic fact in human experience, not as an intrinsic ideal.

To be sure, non-resistance to evil has never been widely practiced, except in the life of small, homogeneous groups. Yet it has been regarded in Christian teachings as representing the highest ethical good.

The ethics of self-abnegation counsels submission to tyranny:

Let every soul be subject to the higher powers.
For there is no power but of God,
The powers that be are ordained of God,
Whosoever therefore resists the power,
Resists the ordinance of God;
And they that resist shall receive to themselves damnation.
— Romans 13:1-4

The classic utterance of Jesus, "Render under Caesar the things that are Caesar's and unto God the things that are God's" (Matthew 22:21; Mark 12:17; Luke 20:25) has been subjected to a vast amount of interpretation. It is generally taken by Christian thinkers to be normative for the relationship of church and state or, alternatively, of religion and society. Whatever other levels of meaning may be found in it, this utterance seems to be in conformity with Paul's elaboration in Romans, cited above, and would seem to express a willingness to accept political tyranny.

The ethics of self-abnegation also urges submission to social inequality, including slavery:

Submit yourselves to every ordinance of man for the Lord's sake, whether it be to the king, as supreme, or unto governors, as unto them that are sent by Him for the punishment of evildoers, and for the praise of them that do well.
— I Peter 2:13-14

That these injunctions were not treated as dead letters is clear from the entire history of the Western world, where the Church was overwhelmingly allied with the secular power in nearly every struggle against tyranny.

Nevertheless, the doctrine of "original sin," eloquently preached in the Epistles of Paul, is by no means identical with the view of man that is expounded in the Hebrew Bible, or even in the Gospels. Nor is it the "plain sense" of the Paradise narrative in Genesis. For Judaism, neither the intent of the biblical text nor the realities of human nature compel us to the doctrine of an ineradicable taint of evil in mankind. In later centuries, the Christian Church recognized this truth. Not only in Pelagianism, which the Christian Church officially rejected, but in the systems of theology which it sanctioned, the doctrine of "original sin" was substantially modified and attenuated. Today the doctrine of "original sin" is not maintained by many, if not by most Christians on the conscious level. However, the pattern of human behavior, perhaps most noticeably in the area of sexual mores, demonstrates how powerful is the hold of this doctrine on the human subconscious. Neither "original sin" nor the ethics of self-abnegation became normative in traditional Judaism. Rabbinic thought, which yielded to no one in its recognition of the elements of imperfection in man, had conceived of man's native endowment as neutral, and saw his instinctual equipment neither as good nor as evil per se, the ultimate judgement upon them depending upon the uses to which they were put. In this worldview, man is a battleground as long as he lives between two impulses, the good impulse (*yetzer hatov*) and the evil impulse (*yetzer hara'*). There is no disposition to underestimate the power of the evil impulse in its manifold forms, but concomitant with it is the recognition that even this impulse can be an instrument for the service of God.

Thus the great biblical injunction: "You shall love the Lord your God with all your heart" bears the rabbinic comment, "with both your impulses, the good and the evil" (Berakot 54a). Anticipating Freud on several counts, the rabbis are fully aware of the power of sexual desire in human life and of its capacity for working havoc with men's lives. They also express their insight that, without this "evil impulse," most of men's functions, such as creative activity, family life and economic pursuits, would cease. According to this approach, human nature is plastic, and any ethical judgement upon its character must follow, not precede, its manifestations in human life.

In sum, for classical New Testament Christianity, man sins because he is a sinner; for traditional Judaism, man is a sinner when he sins.

Rooted in these differing conceptions of human nature are two systems of ethics. While each approach finds expression in both traditions, it is fair to say that one, the ethics of self-abnegation, is central in classical Christianity, while the other, the ethics of self-fulfillment, is basic to normative Judaism. The ethics of self-abnegation finds its clearest expression in the Sermon on the Mount which presents it as the highest ideal of human conduct.

The ethics of self-fulfillment reaches its apogee in the Ten Commandments and in the Golden Rule (Leviticus 19:18), reaffirmed by Hillel and Rabbi Akiba as "the greatest principle of the Torah," while Ben Azzai found it in the test of Genesis 5:1: "This is the book of the generations of Adam; in the day that God created

Adam he fashioned him in the divine image," underscoring both the unity and the dignity of humankind.

A distinguished Christian theologian was asked, "What has contemporary politics to do with the Sermon on the Mount?" To this he replied, and with perfect justice, "Nothing, and it shouldn't." The same categorical negative could not, I believe, have been given to the question, "What has practical politics to do with the Ten Commandments?" For the Decalogue was proclaimed at the beginning of a nation's history; the Sermon on the Mount was believed to usher in the end of history. The former inaugurated the commencement of the significant moral activity of the people of God; the latter announced the conclusion of its group experience in the context of the natural order.

The ethics of self-fulfillment, which finds expression in countless concrete provisions in the Torah, is elaborated upon in the *halakhah* of the Talmud and the Codes. Being intended for a durable society, not likely to disappear overnight, Jewish law, both biblical and rabbinic, is concerned with all the nitty-gritty details of group relations that constitute the framework of human existence. The conduct of husband and wife, parents and children, their mutual duties toward one another, receives considerable attention in the sources. The relations of the individual and the community and their responsibilities to one another are addressed in detail. The conduct of the nation in the world, including the waging of war and the pursuit of peace, occupy an important place in the Torah and the Prophets. The rabbis are aware that in the biblical injunction, "Your brother shall live with you" (Leviticus 25:35), another injunction is also implied: "'With you,' this means that your life comes before that of your fellow" (Baba Mezia 62a). It is realistic in its concept of human nature, recognizing human limitations and potentialities alike. It teaches idealism as its goal, but it demands decency as its minimum. The endless scroll of Jewish heroism and martyrdom through the ages testifies to the capacity of the ethics of self-fulfillment to evoke the noblest acts of self-sacrifice for a cause.

Since life is the supreme good, the ethics of self-fulfillment including its highest manifestation, the act of martyrdom for an ideal goal, finds its justification in the fact that the individual's self-sacrifice ultimately redounds to the enhancement of life for the community. On the other hand, the immolation of a nation or the liquidation of an entire society would have no such beneficial result upon the remainder of humanity. It follows that the only ethic that may legitimately be applied to the group, its aspirations and activities, is the ethics of self-fulfillment, which presupposes self-preservation.

Realistic in its understanding of human nature, the ethics of self-fulfillment stresses concrete deeds rather than abstract emotions and trusts to right actions to lead to proper feelings rather than the reverse. The Sermon on the Mount makes an extreme demand on human nature — comprehensible as an interim ethic — when it proclaims the famous injunction "Love your enemies" (Matthew 5:4). On the other hand, the Book of the Covenant in Exodus (23:4-5) ordains: "If you meet your enemy's ox or his ass going astray, you shall surely bring it back to him again. If you see the ass of your foe lying under its burden, you shall not pass by him, but must release it with him." Rabbinic teaching carries this approach to one's enemies to its conclusion, "Who is a hero, he who makes his foe his friend" (Abot de Rabbi Nathan, ch. 23).

It has not been adequately noted that this strong infusion of realism in the Jewish ethic of self-fulfillment has its source not only in the Torah and the Prophets, but primarily in Wisdom, the third spiritual current in ancient Israel. All too often the ethical contribution of "practical Wisdom" expounded in the Book of Proverbs, *Koheleth* and Ben Sira has been overlooked. An indispensable dimension in biblical ethics is added by the emphasis that the Wisdom writers placed on realism as a virtue and on intelligence as obedience to the will of God. While traditional religious teachers taught that the sinner is a fool, Wisdom declared that the fool is a sinner.

From this conviction two corollaries follow: a course of action, however practical it may seem at the outset, is doomed to failure if it violates the canons of morality; and, conversely, a course of action, however high-minded its aims, is likewise unacceptable if it be unrealistic, because it, too, cannot genuinely advance human well-being.

At last we are able to respond to the question: Is there a difference between the dictates of individual morality and the imperatives that governments and nations must follow? If morality is identified with the ethics of self-abnegation, the answer is clearly in the affirmative — the two patterns of behavior are clearly not compatible. However, if we conceive of morality as an ethic of self-fulfillment, there is no fundamental difference between the demands made on the individual and the standards to which governments should be held.

48

Politics and the Ethics of Judaism

This theoretical conclusion is borne out both by Jewish tradition and by Jewish history. Nowhere in the biblical period, where Jews were masters of their own destiny, living under a government of their choice, did any biblical teacher recognize the dichotomy between the morality applicable to individuals and that practices by governments. Nor does the record disclose any evidence that this argument was made by the practitioners of *realpolitik* in those days. Neither Abraham nor Job, neither Moses nor the Prophets operated with two distinct systems of right and wrong. Similarly, Amos castigated Syria, Moab and Ammon for the physical cruelty they visited upon their conquered enemies and condemned the Phillistines and the Phoenicians for driving their foes into exile. In the "Great Arraignment," Amos applied the same standard to the social sins, the economic inequities, and the sexual immorality rampant within Israel (Amos ch. 1-2).

With the benefit of historical hindsight 2,500 years later, we know that the visionary Prophets and not the practical politicians of the day, the kings and the aristocrats, were the true realists in the international arena. It was Isaiah who urged neutrality in the face of the Assyrian crisis, not Kings Ahaz and Hezekiah, and who was vindicated by the course of events. A century later, the passion of the "patriotic" party at court, and not Jeremiah's counsel opposing rebellion against Babylonia, led to the destruction of the monarchy, the burning of the Temple, and the all-but-complete annihilation of the Jewish people.

For the Prophets and the Bible as a whole, the same standard of good and evil, right and wrong, applied to the behavior of God and man, the individual and the nation. Cruelty and injustice, violence and oppression were violations of the principle which for them was built into the structure of the universe — that right doing leads to well-being and wrong doing to disaster — both in the life of the individual and in affairs of state. This principle, which I have called "the law of consequence" can no more be violated with impunity than any fundamental law in the physical universe.

The rabbis of the Talmudic era had little occasion to meditate on statecraft and apply the principles that should underlie it, but their judgement on the fate of the Roman Empire was entirely of a piece with the prophetic judgement upon the inhumanity and arrogance of Babylonia and Assyria. The medieval commentator who saw in the Pesach song *Had Gadya* a parable of the sin and punishment of the successive empires arising in history, shared with their predecessors the prophetic worldview. He who would argue

49

for dichotomy between the ethics of the individual and the morality of government flies in the face of Jewish tradition; indeed, the tradition would insist that it runs counter to the testimony of human experience and is doomed to failure.

The problems confronting Israel today are tragically complex. The countless solutions that have been proposed must be weighted by the standards of Jewish ethics, resting upon the twin pillars of *tzedek* and *sekhel*, righteousness and wisdom, sympathy and intelligence. What is decisively ruled out is any approach — whether to the Arab-Israel problem or any other — that establishes a dichotomy between politics and morality.

THE CONSEQUENCES OF ACTION TAKEN

Alfred Gottschalk

1. Is there a difference between individual morality and the morality of public policy choices for a state or other political community?

The differences between individual morality and the morality of public policy, or some other entity, arises from the question of consequences from actions taken. It is quite conceivable that an individual could make moral choices outside of community but in relation to another person or persons that remain, by their very definition, individual and consensual. Within this context, an individual's morality and moral or immoral action may or may not touch the community or other entities such as political systems or a state.

Individuals may proceed from the vantage point of an absolutist morality or a relativistic morality. They may have a religious or secular base. There are individual moral acts that are conditioned by one's philosophic point of view and others which are experimentally developed and experienced within one context but not necessarily on other contexts, however congruent they may, at first glance, appear to be.

Individual morality may have broad ranging or limited effects depending upon the experience and context. It is never so with public policy. The choices that a state or other political communities may elect always have consequences for the group. It is under such circumstances that one asks questions such as "Are the actions of an individual or a community reflecting the greatest good for the greatest number?", however the good is to be defined.

Action within community always has consequences and, therefore, what is deemed to be moral or immoral by communal standards eventually becomes the yardstick by which an individual's conduct is measured vis-a-vis others, although such need not be the case with an individual's conduct pursued either in isolation, in which context definitions of morality are irrelevant, or in relation to another person who may consent to conduct which between people may be considered immoral by standards that are not so considered in the smaller consensual relationship. When it is a matter of the morality of public policy, where the choices for a state come into question, a set of standards and values comes into play that has been conditioned by that state or political community by which individuals are measured. In authoritarian societies, such as those that pertain under fascism and under communism, the community may impose a possibly immoral standard upon the individual and may command the individual to comply. Under such circumstances, the individual may or may not have a different moral standard to gauge to the demand for compliance. If he is clearly persuaded that he is asked to do something which he feels to be immoral, he must oppose the state. That feeling can come from an individual's conscience, religious belief, or sheer feelings of empathy for another human being or community of human beings.

2. Assuming a less than perfect world, how should political communities, their leaders and members deal with the problem of maintaining moral positions under duress or at times of crisis?

It is the challenge of leadership and the ultimate determination of the quality of political life how they respond under stress or duress or in times of crisis. This is when the mettle of an individual or a society is tested. Moral responses under such conditions require innate courage, tensile strength fashioned from firm convictions of right and wrong, and the willingness to suffer consequences for moral positions held against the requirements or the demands of state or an autocratic, authoritarian community.

In our time we have seen the challenge to conscience from societies that have required individuals to abuse, denigrate or murder others in the pursuit of a national goal or policy. Witness the dehumanization that took place during the Nazi period of millions of Europeans who were involved in the conspiracy to annihilate six million Jews as well as other minorities or dissenting groups. Failure of nerve and conscience marked this period. One can claim such episodes in human history as evincing the failure of human civilization or in this instance, European civilization, to withstand the call to commit atrocities by an intransigent Nazi state that for its fulfillment required the annihilation of those who stood in opposition to it. Those who complied lost their moral compass, never to regain it. They surrendered their humanistic or

Christian values and permitted the bestial elements in human nature to triumph.

To maintain moral positions under stress or times of crisis, other than those I have just alluded to, requires the capacity to fine tune one's action to one's basic commitments, to one's understanding of moral obligation and the question of the "ought" in human conduct. One may, from time to time, be required to compromise, "in this less than perfect world," but never to surrender one's intrinsic beliefs of right and wrong.

3. To what extent does or should a morally relativistic or morally absolutist position influence one's conclusions with regard to the first two questions?

The most equivocal but probably the most realistic moral conduct that can be gauged within the consensual frame is that of relativistic morality. Relativistic morality requires that the individuals evaluating one another's acts come to a common understanding of what is harmful or beneficial to the other. It is solely determined, in most instances, by a standard that does not appeal to an absolute category of right and wrong and consequently is much more difficult to gauge except by its results and the quality of the relationship that is maintained by virtue of the conduct exercised.

An absolutist position is usually arbitrary and judgmental, fixing definitions of right and wrong by some preexisting standard against which human conduct in its individual or communal sense is measured. In Judaism the Ten Commandments come within this category because they are apodictic and not casuistic. Each statement is not questionable in relational circumstances. It is either prohibited or commanded conduct. Expected orthodox behavior emanating from commanded conduct is easily measured by the preexisting standard of the commander but may be much more difficult to live out in a society that requires mutual consent to what is right and wrong, except, of course, where an entire society or state assumes an absolutist standard against which all behavior is measured. We have seen how such states and political communities as well as religious entities have ended in the kinds of absolute systems that lead to "Khomeinism" or orthodoxies of other kinds based on revelation if they are religious or the kind of apodictic teaching that has pertained in communism and other political systems where what is right and wrong is determined by the absolutist policy of the party or state.

I am committed to a humanistic, morally relativistic society which adapts from the collective wisdom of civilization those standards by which people can live and affirm human life in dignity and responsibility. It is a safer system than the absolutist systems which have oppressed humankind over the centuries and from which, when one is ensnared, it is virtually impossible to escape except through new revolutions and more bloodshed. Enlightened morality should be agreed upon through consensus so that we can achieve the greatest good for the greatest number.

INTELLIGENCE, MORALITY, AND FOREIGN POLICY

Sidney Hook

There are at least three fundamental questions whose answers have a direct bearing on the conduct and outcome of any intelligent foreign policy. The first is whether the normal political process can cope effectively with the problems and perennial crises of foreign policy, or whether this is a domain in which ultimate decisions must be entrusted to a dedicated corps of trained specialists responsible only to the executive power. The second is whether principles of morality can and should operate in guiding the conduct of foreign policy, and to what extent the national interest should be subordinated to such principles when their role is acknowledged. The third is what moral choices are open to a democratic nation like our own in a world in which it is threatened by aggressive totalitarian powers and ideologies.

From de Tocqueville to Walter Lippmann democracies have been faulted because of their inability to conduct intelligent foreign policies. The argument is quite familiar. Where domestic policies are concerned their fruits can be roughly but properly determined by consequences perceived not too long after they have been adopted. If unsatisfactory, they can be corrected or agitation against them developed. But the consequences of a foreign policy are rarely immediate. Critical judgment usually follows only after the experience of bitter fruits of disaster. On the other hand, where the urgencies of a crisis situation require immediate response the democratic process is too slow and unwieldy. It is therefore concluded that because of the delicacy, complexity, and sometimes the necessary secrecy of foreign policy, negotiations and actions cannot be subjected to public discussion. The strategies to meet acts of foreign aggression must be initiated before their outcome confronts the nation and limits its choice of alternatives of response. There is great danger to the national interest — today even to national survival — in deferring to the vagaries of public opinion that tend to swing pendularly from one extreme to another. De Tocqueville's words are often cited to drive these points home. "Foreign politics demand scarcely any of those qualities which a democracy possesses; and they require, on the contrary, the perfect use of almost all those faculties in which it is deficient....A democracy is unable to regulate the details of an important undertaking, to persevere in a design, and to work out its execution in the presence of serious obstacles. It cannot combine its measures with secrecy, and it will not await their consequences with patience."

De Tocqueville's indictment can be substantiated from the historical record. When memories of past wars are faint, public opinion can too easily be aroused in support of armed conflict. This was apparent in 1914. And once hostilities begin, the slogans of total victory or unconditional surrender become extremely popular. Proposals for a negotiated peace are denounced as treasonable. On the other hand, after a costly war popular opinion is apt to become fearful and defeatist and to resist policies which, had they been adopted in time, might have prevented the very outcome that was feared most. The popular opposition to the rearmament of Britain in the 1930s is a case in point. Another is the failure to act vigorously against Hitler's reentry into the Rhineland in defiance of the Treaty of Versailles. And although it is often ignored, the capitulation to Hitler at Munich was approved with wild popular enthusiasm as insuring peace in our time.

PUBLIC MORALITY AS TRYING TO BE HONEST

Philip M. Klutznick

First of all, what constitutes morality in a given situation may itself be debatable. Secondly, in a response from one who has served in city, state, national and international political organizations, my attitude is necessarily influenced by that experience.

By the nature of the comparison called upon, the simple answer has to be that there are instances in which there is a difference between individual morality and the morality of public policy choices for a public body of any kind. The nature of the position of an individual and the state or other political community may compel that difference. As an individual, one can decide for oneself what is moral or immoral. When as an individual one participates in public policy choices for a state or other political community, it is only rarely when one is the final arbiter of the decision that an individual can act as if he alone must make the decision. There are others in authority, unless one is the head of state or a community, who are called upon to join in a consideration of what is or is not moral in a real sense.

The suggestion that one assume a less than perfect world is, of course, surplusage. The very character of the world is such that for it to be perfect would almost be self-destructive. The world is made up of all types and kinds of people with varying degrees of civilization and background. I introduce this statement as appropriate to the question of how should political communities, their leaders and members deal with the problem of maintaining moral positions under duress at times of crisis. Once again what I referred to as the definition of morality or morality of public policy in the prior paragraph becomes even more complex and difficult when the issue is looked at in universal dimensions. This question is almost unanswerable in terms of an effective guideline. As one who has worked in international affairs not only in the general community but in public life and public responsibility, the first lesson that one has to learn is that there is more than one honorable and decent side to almost every international question depending upon who is making the decision and from where they come and what their historic background and present situation may be. It would be my view that absolutism and adequate definitions of what is a moral position to be maintained under duress is almost a matter of negotiation as between the parties involved in that moral duress. That there should be honorable intentions based upon the concepts of a particular society is beyond question. But, what constitutes honorable intentions can meaningfully vary as between the peoples of different origination, background and environment. The oversimplification of what is moral in terms of the universe has created some of the most immoral conflicts in history. If I were asked to pin down my belief, I would have to say that moral questions in a universal sense require that the parties to any dispute have a full and complete appreciation for the differences in the mores of the contending parties. Then having that understanding in an effort to maintain tranquility and mutuality, the parties involved of different backgrounds must strive to achieve an accommodation which honors and respects each other's concept of morality. Generalizations in my experience have limited application to the complex and varied universe that man has inherited.

My answer as to the extent that morally relativistic or morally absolutist positions do or should influence one's conclusion is almost self-evident in the response to the first two questions. Generally speaking, when there are differences, morally relativistic or absolute, there is something in the moral background of nearly all peoples with whom I have been related throughout the world that permits for the accommodation as long as it is honestly held of differing moral positions.

It may be that I have not gotten the right interpretation of what all three of these questions are meant to uncover. I am reminded of my last conversations with the late Dr. Mordecai Kaplan when he was already 103. At one point when three of us were sitting with him, one of us asked him if he had a good word for us. Despite his feeble condition at 103 plus, after considerable thought he said, "I have loved the Jewish people throughout my life because during the peoples' life they have always tried to be honest." I would suggest that the best answer to all these questions is for each of the states, communities and individuals, whether one nation or many nations, to try to be honest to what they believe themselves and honest in the approach in consideration of what others may believe.

MORALITY AND DECISIONS OF STATE

Samuel Krislov

Only at the extremes are these basic questions consensually answerable. When, for example, President Kennedy sought to deal with the Cuban crisis, the White House announced he was ill, giving him time to cancel appointments and consider options. No one has suggested this was a deviation from morality though such a minor lie in commercial affairs might raise an eyebrow, and if used in personal matters — to gain sympathy for seductive purposes, for example — might be seen as a breach of faith. Indeed, in spite of the coupling of love and war as areas where "all's fair," the standards are decisively different. The Bible chronicles all sorts of deceitful military maneuvers, from Gideon's breaking of pitchers to simulate large numbers of soldiers or Judith's killing the tyrant in bed, all with seeming approval if not downright admiration. By and large, history mimics the Bible in its plaudits for dissembling for the collective good, particularly during the clash of arms.

Conversely there are limits beyond which nearly universal disapproval sets in. The Japanese treatment of the Koreans, and the viciousness of the Pol Pot regime are all seen not merely as examples of cruelty, but as examples of humankind's peculiar ability to forget about others whenever it suits them.

Hans J. Morgenthau was the strongest advocate in political science of "power politics" and "national interest" as the true test of foreign policy. He authored several books repudiating ethics and morality, on the one hand, or international efficiency — "scientific man," on the other, as the building blocks for a nation-state's conduct in foreign affairs. But when A.J.P. Taylor wrote a book arguing that Hitler was best analyzed not as a terrible figure contaminating the second quarter of the twentieth century but merely as a German statesman furthering traditional German goals by non-traditional means — extermination of entire populations — Morgenthau was no more supportive of Taylor than more moralistic analysts. Perhaps because he himself was a refugee, but more essentially because of his sense of humanity, Morgenthau did not leap to defend the argument — a reasonable extension of his own thesis — that one judged a state merely by the logic of its goals, and that such a goal could be pursued by any means whatsoever.

In short, I do not believe anyone has rigorously argued or acted on either extreme form of the proposition that personal morality is isomorphic with state morality or that conversely there is no overlap at all. Rather, there is a muddied sense that the relationship is complex and not easily captured.

It does not seem to me that the essence of any important problem lies in the espousal or non-espousal of a relativist ethic. In general, real-life statesmen generally face complex situations involving conflicting ethics rather than neat tests of one standard. Generally moralists with an operative strict philosophy are quickly eliminated from office much as Jehovah's Witnesses could not survive long in concentration camps. Political survivors who espouse a rigid philosophy generally also possess strong systems of rationalization which allow them to notice facts bringing a situation under one set of ethical considerations and ignoring contrary evidence. Thus John Foster Dulles or President McKinley could extract unequivocal conclusions from highly equivocal information and overlook facts others saw as inescapable. Still another practical triumph over conviction can be extracted from delegating implementation to subordinates not somehow seen as confined by the same principles, therefore permitted to deviate from ethics without compromising the soul of the supposed decision-maker. In its purist form it is represented by a not-uncommon use of non-Moslems to handle foreign affairs and aspects of banking in Islamic states so that impure actions represent the burden of these infidels. This is the state-level version of the *Shabbos goy*, the non-Jew who by arrangement does tasks forbidden to the observant. Most espionage systems operate in parallel to this, and can be managed at the highest level by individuals who would theoretically deplore the details but who take care they do not hear what they do not want to know.

Rather than the sense of moral relativism or absolute relativism in a philosophical sense, what seems to me powerfully operative is a sociological imperative that is the degree to which some value is perceived as universalistic both within the nation-state and as among its rival partners interacting internationally. Decision-makers find themselves in a quandary under any circumstances but especially in a situation of diverse values within a society. They cannot then easily act in accordance with their most squeamish values, for they are no longer individuals but fiduciaries with profound responsibility to others. By obeying their finest impulses they may endanger the society and the members thereof. An individual may easily resolve such problems and run such a risk for himself or herself and be esteemed ethically, but one who assumes the right to risk the fate of others is in a much more ambiguous position. Bacon pointed out that one who chooses to raise a family has "given hostages to fortune." The undertaking of state office is to give hostages to a myriad of influences.

The essential, real and inevitable dilemma posited here can (and is) exploited psychologically by the average statesman and serves to permit wide-scale amorality. The dilemma is inevitable, even in a state nominally in agreement on its value system, as e.g., a Moslem state. Even here there will be a range of absolutist versus flexible attitudes within the society, a greater or lesser attention to the nuances of the system, though the range of disagreement will be reduced. (If "everyone" agrees, the decision-maker is not imposing merely personal values.) Similarly the question of whether the highest level of ethics should be applied in dealing with an interacting collectivity will vary in terms of both the actor-nation's value system and its appreciation of the worthiness of the other. Actions are in part determined by the sense in which the recipient is seen as bound by the same value system. (Civilized collectivities should be treated civilly, and the risk is less they will abuse good treatment or mistake it for weakness.)

Because there is such wide latitude on both these scores it is normally easy enough to argue that a range of action foreclosed to a moral actor on his or her own behalf, a personally immoral decision, is in fact required on a fiduciary basis on behalf of others. The sin, as it were, is deflected back to the collectivity, and pragmatic, not moral, decisions will prevail. Even during a town meeting situation unborn generations, or already born immature members of the society, will be invoked in the same way; you must do this on their unrepresented behalf though repugnant to all of us here.

These absolutions operate within limits set in part by the society's value system — there are things so horrendous, e.g., Greeks will not do — or its own historical experience. (We do not do that because we tried it and it did us damage, or we do not mistreat aliens "for you were strangers in Egypt.")

What complicates this easy justification for amoral statecraft is the advantage that accrues to moral actors. The pope has the equivalent of many divisions as General Jaruzelski will verify. Machiavelli argued that it is merely the appearance or perception of virtue that was significant and no doubt that is the bottom line. But since observers are not universally fools, the perception that a state behaves ethically correlates highly with its actual behavior.

There is something off-putting and pollyannish about Adolf Berle's argument that there is a *Natural Selection of Political Forces* favoring moral and altruistic values. Certainly history indicates clearly that nice guys finish last enough of the time to make Durocher's law as plausible as Berle's.

Still an honorable reputation is an asset, and probably a greater asset than one for ruthlessness. The Reagan administration came into office expressing contempt for the Carter administration's sentimentalism over human rights. It will leave office having pursued that program as vigorously as its predecessor, having come to appreciate this value as an instrument of foreign policy. (The fact that the program also had domestic political appeal to traditionally Democratic voters of Eastern European origins did not hurt, but that was lagniappe.)

Universalistic values have political appeal. Athens could attract allies more easily than Sparta, the U.S. more than a Stalinist USSR. So a society can *instrumentally* evaluate its adherence or rejection of ethical standards both with respect to its goals and its means.

This is at least as important a force as the individual consciences of decision-makers or of the collective social attitude of the whole society. Whether a major power or a minor player, a nation must realize its reputation is influenced by its behavior and its perceived level of ethics.

All of this has implications for Israel, some clear, others murky. As a newly-minted nation, one with self-conscious creation as a society built on principle and attracting populations on its principled values, it has a special need to evaluate its existence and its conduct with respect to ethical standards. Arguably the acceptance of Israel as a true nation-state will only be achieved when it is judged by the same ruthless amoralism that, say, Iraq is expected to live up to — a sort of extension of Bialek's charming response to the spread of prostitution in Palestine: "at last we have become a nation among nations." But that date has not yet arrived. Israel makes special claims as to its merits; it cannot shrug off criticism holding it to a high standard.

It is generally assumed that rabbinic Judaism is an absolute system of morality. In point of fact, *halakhah* is extremely flexible, particularly when the value of community existence is at stake. One may fight an enemy on the Sabbath if that is required. Most precepts can be set aside "to live by them, not to die by them." Setting limits to this situational flexibility are clear examples of gross immorality: murder or homicide to save oneself ("how do you know your blood is redder than your brother's"), idolatry, or gross ethical misconduct. The emphasis upon survival is carried to the point of authorizing emergency community control beyond *halakhah* if needed. Perhaps the finest epitome of this basic attitude is found in Peretz's story "Three Who Ate" of the rabbinic leadership in the face of a plague requiring the community to eat on Yom Kippur, and themselves beginning the process with tears in their eyes, eating before the assembled community.

Perhaps a quarter of the Israeli community is Orthodox (*dati*), with a large but indefinite number deeply influenced by that value system as opposed to ritual requirements of the religion (*masorti*). This had deep vestigial influence even among the "secular" socialists who constitute the core of the left (and are in many ways the elite privileged ruling class of the society even though now outvoted at the polls), or the urban anti-socialist professionals and middle-class business types who are the leadership core of the right. They are deeply committed to historical traditions on fair treatment and ethical conduct, but as ideologues strongly involved in continued development of their nation-state, which they or their parents helped launch.

There is, then, as much or more agreement on priority of values in Israel as in most modern states. It emerges rather more loosely than assumed from Judaic values, as Israel is much less directly religious than is naively assumed abroad, but it is also more pervasively influenced by Judaism than cynical surface observation would detect. It is also much more defensive and survival-conscious because the Holocaust and Masada are only manifestations of a strand of history, of repeated dangers and threats. The Sephardim did not share in the Holocaust but understood Begin's evocation of it all too well. This memory places a premium on community survival, which may well be the core of Judaism. (Even the greatest saint requires nine others to permit the full system of prayer in a *minyan*.)

Given this value system and the geo-political and military situation in the Middle East, there is a core of understanding among the contestants in Israel on basics, except for small groups roughly comparable to Holy Rollers, on one side, and unblinking pacifists, on the other. "Even Israel's doves are half-hawks" complained a trendy visitor in the 1960s to me. Understandably, total withdrawal from Vietnam by U.S. forces presents a different level of issue from total withdrawal from the West Bank and Gaza.

It is within this priority of continuity that the ethical battle in Israel takes place. And the Israeli debate is largely voiced not so much in terms of what conduct Jews owe Arabs, but even more about the corrosive effects such conduct has on the Jewish community. This is partly tactical since the debate is aimed at winning over the unaligned. There is also a major issue of how that community is to be regarded abroad, but Israelis have had that issue raised about so many things, big and little, that its specter has little actual impact on their own attitudes. Ultimately the argument boils down to what risks one is willing to undertake: clear erosion of ethical standards and loss of regard by the world community as opposed to sacrifice of military position. Israel has been quite forthcoming and even self-sacrificing in some aspects and may not appreciate how much it has benefited from those concessions. At other times it has run roughshod over ethical and popularity considerations and usually has done so without obvious backlash and threatened costs. (Lebanon is the conspicuous exception, and the *intifada* on the West Bank may be another.) How one balances these considerations is influenced partly by the depth of one's ethical commitments, but even more by one's sense of history and destiny.

In the past few months I have reluctantly come to join those who conclude that Israel has learned the wrong lessons from its experience of the last quarter century, is on a wrong course, and is losing its soul. Survival is assumed to be primarily a geo-military consideration involving manipulation of others rather than one emerging from self-development and self-reliance. This is not a comforting thought and my only consolation is that I have been wrong before and hopefully have misdiagnosed this situation I feel so profoundly — morally and practically — involved with.

MORAL CONTROL OF POWER THROUGH THE RULE OF LAW

Moshe Landau

How do we solve the grave dilemma between the vital need to preserve the very existence of the state and its citizens and maintain its character as a law-abiding state which believes in basic moral principles? The law, which expresses the will of a free people, is the keystone for the existence of a state such as ours, which believes in values of liberty and equality.

If we do not preserve the rule of law zealously, the danger is great that the work of those who assail the existence of the state from without will be done through acts of self-destruction from within, with "men devouring each other." If the government needs scope for its operations in addition to what the law of the land allows, the solution lies in convincing the legislator that the law should be amended, not in disregarding the existing law.

At the hearing in the Supreme Court of Israel of an appeal by Izzat Nafsu, an officer in the Israel Defense Forces, against his conviction on charges of treason, espionage and aiding the enemy during wartime, it transpired that during the interrogation of Nafsu preceding his trial he had been subjected to physical violence by interrogators of the General Security Service (GSS), who had then given false evidence during his trial. Following these revelations the government of Israel resolved on 31 May 1987 to set up a Commission of Enquiry on "investigation methods and procedures of the GSS on Hostile Terrorist Activity (HTA) and the giving of evidence in court in connection with such investigations."

According to the Commissions of Enquiry Law, 1968, the President of the Supreme Court then appointed this writer (a former President of the Supreme Court) to be Chairman, and Ya'akov Malz (the then-State Comptroller) and Major General (ret.) Yitzhak Hofi to be members of the Commission. The Commission issued its report on 30 October 1987, the recommendations of which were later adopted in full by the government of Israel.

In its consideration of the Nafsu case, the Commission had to carefully address the moral dilemmas involved in the exercise of power by the state security services, especially focusing on the use of state power in the interrogation of those suspected of hostile terrorist activity.

Jurists have generally recognized the legitimacy of the actions of one who performs an act which he believes is immediately necessary, in order to prevent death or serious injury to himself or others, when the danger he believes exists is of such a nature that it would have been impossible to demand of him to act otherwise.

The Israeli Penal Code exempts from criminal responsibility an individual who acts in obedience to an order given by a competent authority, provided that the order was not manifestly illegal; "manifestly illegal" meaning that any person of conscience will see a black flag saying "prohibited" flying over such an order.

According to Sec. 22 of the Israeli Penal Code:

A person may be exempted from criminal responsibility for an act or omission if he can show that it was done or made in order to avoid consequences which could not otherwise be avoided and which would have inflicted grievous harm or injury on his person, honor or property or on the person or honor of others whom he was bound to protect or on property placed in his charge, provided that he did no more than was reasonably necessary for that purpose and that the harm caused by him was not disproportionate to the harm avoided.

This section allows those in authority to take action for the protection of others, provided three cumulative conditions have been fulfilled:

1. That the individual acted in order to prevent grievous harm to his person or honor or to the person of others whom he was bound to protect or to property placed in his charge.
2. That this harm could not otherwise have been avoided.
3. That he did no more than was reasonably necessary for that purpose and that the harm caused thereby was not disproportionate in the circumstances of the case.

The section accords the perpetrator of the act full exemption from criminal responsibility, and does not confine itself to formal conviction with mitigation of punishment. It reflects the clash of opposing values: on the one hand, values protected by means of the prohibitions of criminal law, and on the other hand, the duty, grounded in ethical precepts, to protect one's life or bodily integrity or that of others. Like the defense of obedience to orders, the law confronts this dilemma of the impossibility of reaching an absolute reconciliation between these two values purely by means of formal law, and thus it foregoes the attempt to solve the problem only by these means, and breaches, as it were, the barrier of judicial categories, and appeals to the sense of legality innate in the conscience of every human being. In other words, the law itself deviates under these circumstances from the framework of the criminal prohibitions laid down by law, for the sake of preserving a human value which is of higher importance than implementing these prohibitions.

In the case of the interrogation of a suspect by a GSS investigator, during which the investigator performs an act or makes an omission, such as an injury to the person or well-being of the suspect, or a threat to him, which contain elements of a criminal offense, the harm done by violating a provision of the law during an interrogation must be weighed against the harm to the life or person of others which could occur sooner or later.

Prof. Paul H. Robinson of Rutgers University discussed this choice in his monograph on *Criminal Law Defenses*, in which he gave the following example:

> Suppose a ship's crew discovers a slow leak soon after leaving port. The captain unreasonably refuses to return to shore. The crew must mutiny in order to save themselves and the passengers. If the leak would not pose an actual danger of capsizing the vessel for two days, should its crew be forced to wait until the danger is imminent, even though the disabled ship will be too far out at sea to reach shore when it is? Or should they be able to act before it is too late, even though it may be several days before the danger of capsizing is present?

Or, in an additional example by Robinson:

> Consider the case of the bombmaker X, whose construction plans require a 10-day period for building the weapon. Suppose further that the actor, D, knows that X is going to set off the bomb in a school. He also knows that X's construction plans require 10 days to build the weapon, and that police and other authorities are unavailable to intervene. Under the simple requirement that the conduct be "necessary," the actor could trespass on X's property and abort the plan by disabling the bomb at any time, including the first day, as long as such an

action was the least drastic means of preventing the project's completion. Under the "immediately necessary" restriction, the actor would be obliged to wait until the last day, presumably until the last moment that intervention would still be effective.

Here, the author comments that the second alternative is justified only to enable A to abandon his scheme in the meantime; however, many legislators would prefer to protect society at the cost of earlier intervention against one plotting such a scheme.

The Commission was in accord with these remarks. They are consistent with the wording of the statutory provision which, as stated, makes no mention of any particular requirement for the imminence of the danger, but posits instead the flexible test of "the concept of the lesser evil."

Regarding the first condition required by Sec. 22 of the Penal Code, the information which an interrogator can obtain from the suspect, about caches of explosive materials in the possession or knowledge of the suspect, about acts of terrorism which are about to be perpetrated, about the members of a terrorist group to which he belongs, about the headquarters of terrorist organizations inside the country or abroad, and about terrorist training camps — any such information can prevent mass killing and individual terrorist acts which are about to be carried out. GSS investigators are charged with the task of protecting the citizenry against this as part of their official tasks. It is a salient security interest of the state to protect the lives of its citizens, and the duty to defend them, imposed on the state, certainly falls within the category of the need to prevent bodily harm or grievous injury.

The second condition embodied in Sec. 22 is that it was impossible to prevent the anticipated harm in any other way. It has already been explained above, in regard to GSS interrogations, that the information possessed by a member of a terrorist organization (or a member of a group of local persons which has organized at its own initiative to perpetrate acts of terrorism) cannot be uncovered except through the interrogation of persons concerning whom the GSS has previous information about their affiliation with such an organization or group; we also saw that without some such previous information the GSS does not commence the interrogation of a suspect. Without such an interrogation there is no way to get to the arms caches and explosive materials stores, the location of which is a secret known only to the suspect and the members of his group

— and only he can reveal information about fellow members of his group to his interrogators.

The third condition is that, for the purpose of obtaining this information, the interrogator did not do more than was reasonably necessary and did not thereby cause disproportionate harm under the circumstances. This condition should be considered in light of "the concept of the lesser evil," which was noted earlier. In an article by Adrian A.S. Zuckerman of Oxford University published in the *Law Quarterly Review* (January 1986) entitled "The Right against Self-Incrimination: An Obstacle to the Supervision of Interrogation," he discussed the inadmissibility of a confession obtained by beating a person interrogated:

> This is not to say that it is impossible to envisage situations where the organs of the state may excusably resort to torture. Where it is known that a bomb has been planted in a crowded building, it is perhaps justifiable to torture the suspect so that lives may be saved by discovering its location.

This is an extreme example of actual torture, the use of which would perhaps be justified in order to uncover a bomb about to explode in a building full of people. Under such circumstances, the danger is indeed imminent. However, according to the examples from Prof. Robinson's monograph cited above, vigorous action to prevent the danger of loss of life is also justified, even though the danger will only be realized in the course of time. And indeed, when the clock wired to the explosive charge is already ticking, what difference does it make, in terms of the necessity to act, whether the charge is certain to be detonated in five minutes or in five days? The deciding factor is not the element of time, but the comparison between the gravity of the two evils — the evil of contravening the law as opposed to the evil which will occur sooner or later. As was already stated above, weighing these two evils, one against the other, must be performed according to the concepts of morality implanted in the heart of every decent and honest person. To put it bluntly, the alternative is: are we to accept the offense of assault entailed in slapping a suspect's face or threatening him in order to induce him to talk and reveal a cache of explosive materials meant for use in carrying out an act of mass terror against a civilian population, and thereby prevent the greater evil which is about to occur? The answer is self-evident.

It is true that strict care must be taken, lest a breach of the structure of prohibitions of the criminal law bring about a loosening of the reins, with each interrogator taking matters into his own hands through the unbridled, arbitrary use of coercion against a suspect. In this way the image of the state as a law-abiding polity which preserves the rights of the citizen is liable to be irreparably perverted, with it coming to resemble those regimes which grant their security organs unbridled power. In order to meet this danger, several measures must be taken: first, disproportionate exertion of pressure on the suspect is inadmissible; the pressure must never reach the level of physical torture or maltreatment of the suspect or grievous harm to his honor which deprives him of his human dignity. Second, the possible use of less serious measures must be weighed against the degree of anticipated danger, according to the information in the possession of the interrogator. Third, the physical and psychological means of pressure permitted for use by an interrogator must be defined and limited in advance, by issuing binding directives. Fourth, there must be strict supervision of the implementation in practice of the directives given to GSS interrogators. Fifth, the interrogator's superiors must react firmly and without hesitation to every deviation from the permissible, imposing disciplinary punishment, and in serious cases by causing criminal proceedings to be instituted against the offending interrogator.

A state which believes in liberal principles must face cruel dilemmas in the war against terrorism which threatens its existence. As Professor Paul Wilkinson of Aberdeen University, Scotland, wrote in *Terrorism and the Liberal State*:

> Internal terrorism is after all a particularly barbaric form of unconventional war and political leaders and decision-makers may need to make tough and unpleasant decisions to safeguard the security of state and citizens....In the final analysis terrorists are engaged in a test of will with the democratic community and its leaders....
>
> Ultimately the liberal state has no deus ex machina it can rely upon to rescue it from the agonizing political and moral dilemmas of waging war on terrorism. In the end each sovereign liberal state is left to shift as best it can in the constant struggle to uphold the rule of law and to protect the life and limb of its citizens.

Three ways exist for solving this grave dilemma between the vital need to preserve the very existence of the state and its citizens and to maintain its character as a law-abiding state which believes in basic moral principles, for the methods of police interrogation which are employed in any given regime are a faithful mirror of the character of the entire regime.

The first way proposed is to recognize that because of crucial interests of state security, the activity of the Security Services in their war against terrorism occurs in a "twilight zone" which is outside the realm of the law, and therefore these services should be freed from the bonds of the law and must be permitted deviations from the law.

This way must be utterly rejected. The law, which expresses the will of a free people, is the keystone for the existence of a state such as ours, which believes in values of liberty and equality. If the GSS, with its immense latent power, is not to be subject to the rule of law in its interrogations, who will determine its modes in such cases? Will it run itself or will the political echelon regulate for it its own set of laws? It is quite obvious that if this way is followed, control over the GSS is one day liable to fall into the hands of an unscrupulous person or group of persons, and from there to the despotism of a police state is but a hair's breadth. If we do not preserve the rule of law zealously in this area as well, the danger is great that the work of those who assail the existence of the state from without will be done through acts of self-destruction from within: a veritable "war of all against all." If the GSS needs room for operation in addition to what the law of the land allows, the solution lies in convincing the legislators that the law should be amended, not in disregarding the existing law.

A version slightly different from the above would have the GSS be subordinate to its own quasi-legal system, parallel to but separate from the laws of the country, with the GSS setting up its own internal law and justice, and scrupulously preserving that internal law on its own, while imposing discipline and, when the need arises, punitive sanctions, on its own personnel. The Commission saw that this path led the GSS into a dead end from which it must extricate itself and embark on a road of full obedience to the laws of the state where its methods of interrogation are concerned.

The second way is that of hypocrites: they declare that they abide by the rule of law, but turn a blind eye to what goes on beneath the surface. A salient description of this frame of mind is found in an article by Prof. Joseph W. Bishop, Jr., of Yale University, "Control of Terrorism and Insurrection: The British Laboratory Experience" [in *Law and Contemporary Problems*, vol. 42 (1978),

Duke University]. Referring to harsh methods of interrogation, the author noted: "The inclination of the average, ordinarily humanitarian, Member of Parliament (or Congressman, or voter) is to tolerate the use of such methods, but only when they are 'unbeknownst' to him."

Or, in the figurative language of one of the GSS witnesses: "It is convenient for the citizen to sit on the clean green grass in front of his house, while beneath him the refuse is washed away in the sewerage pipes." But the comparison is not apt, because it is impossible to isolate any one state authority from the overall social structure, and rot in one place is liable to spread and engulf the entire structure.

It is unavoidable to opt for the third way — the road of the truth of the rule of law — even where this difficult subject, too, is concerned. The law itself must ensure a proper framework for the activity of the GSS regarding Hostile Terrorist Activity (HTA) interrogations, with all the attendant problems and dilemmas. The Commission was convinced that this is essential for the moral resilience of Israeli society and of the GSS as a part thereof.

Acts of terrorism have as their aim the deprivation of a basic right of all citizens, namely, the right to life and to physical wellbeing. Organizations which set this as their goal have no moral right to demand that the state for its part maintain towards them the conventional civil rights. Nevertheless, it is incumbent upon the state and its authorities, including the GSS, to preserve humanitarian behavior and human dignity in their treatment of terrorists, in order to uphold the credo of the country itself as a lawabiding state grounded in fundamental concepts of morality. Any infringement of these basic concepts, even vis-a-vis those who would destroy the state, is liable to recoil on us by engendering internal moral corruption.

The Commission is convinced that effective activity by the GSS to thwart terrorist acts is impossible without use of the tool of the interrogation of suspects, in order to extract from them vital information known only to them and unobtainable via other methods. The effective interrogation of terrorist suspects is impossible without the use of means of pressure in order to overcome an obdurate will not to disclose information and to overcome the fear of the person under interrogation that harm will befall him from his own organization if he does reveal information. Interrogation of this kind is permissible under the law, and a confession thus obtained is admissible in a criminal trial, under the existing rulings of the Supreme Court.

The means of pressure should principally take the form of non-violent psychological pressure through a vigorous and extensive interrogation, with the use of stratagems, including acts of deception. However, when these do not attain their purpose, the exertion of a moderate measure of physical pressure cannot be avoided. GSS interrogators should be guided by setting clear boundaries in this matter, in order to prevent the use of inordinate physical pressure arbitrarily administered by the interrogator. Guidelines concerning such boundaries have existed in the Service ever since the scope of investigation of HTA was expanded, as required by the new situation following the Six-Day War. These guidelines underwent occasional changes, generally in the direction of restrictions on the use of physical force, which were imposed from time to time at the initiative of the political echelon, until today the authorization of physical contact with the person under interrogation is extremely limited.

In the second (secret) part of the Commission's report, the Commission formulated a new code of guidelines for GSS interrogators which define, on the basis of past experience, and with as much precision as possible, the boundaries of what is permitted to the interrogator and mainly what is prohibited to him. The Commission was convinced that if these boundaries are maintained exactly in letter and in spirit, the effectiveness of the interrogation will be assured, while at the same time it will be far from the use of physical or mental torture, maltreatment of the person being interrogated, or the degradation of his human dignity.

ON HILLEL, KANT AND THE *INTIFADA*

Netanel Lorch

The field of ethics is reserved for, or monopolized by philosophers, social scientists and theologians in its descriptive aspects; by priests, rabbis and writers in its prescriptive ones. The present writer is none of these. His modest contribution is that of an historian; a former soldier, diplomat and public servant; of a Jew who is interested, an Israeli who is concerned.

Hillel the Elder's dictum: "what you detest, do not inflict it on others," refined, if you will, in Kant's categorical imperative, namely: "act on maxims which can at the same time have for their objects themselves as universal laws of nature"; in other words: act in such a manner that your actions can serve as the yardstick for the actions of others; that, I believe, is the basis of all morality, whether humanist or deist, ancient or modern. The fact, abundantly illustrated, that morals change with the times — *mores* change with the change of *tempore* — that generations and cultures, societies and groups within societies differ from each other in their *precise* definition of what, for a given generation, culture or society, constitutes such action, does not detract from the validity and the universal applicability of Hillel or Kant.

What is true of individuals is true of societies. These consist of, are represented by and act through individuals. Our generation, perhaps more than any other, has experienced and observed the results of a divorce between public and private morality: the faithful husbands who belonged to *Einsatzgruppen*; the passionate animal lovers who serviced gas ovens in which thousands of children perished. True, there is a *raison d'etat* which endows the state with special faculties, and it has moral validity. It is no more far-reaching than the principle of *"haba lehorgecha"* for the individual. The individual is permitted — moreover, in Jewish law is obliged — to anticipate the one who comes to slay him; similarly the state has the right, nay, the obligation towards its citizens to defend itself and them, to use them in order to defend itself.

An order which, prima facie, runs counter to legal norms or to accepted moral precepts does not obligate its recipient, whatever his position in a given hierarchy; on the contrary, its

75

implementation may in itself constitute an immoral, illegal, punishable act. This principle has been at the root of many of the postwar and post-Holocaust trials. It has been pronounced by an Israeli court in the Kfar Kassim trial of 1957. It is consonant with both Hillel and Kant.

This imposes a heavy burden on those who on behalf of the state are entitled to issue orders. For them the maxim should read: Your instructions to others should be issued in such a manner that those receiving and implementing them, and those who honestly believe that this is what they are doing, will be following moral precepts, will be perceived by others to be following them, will be spared the dilemma, the agony of deciding for themselves whether or not they are indeed acting in a morally defensible way.

Whenever a soldier is found guilty, through due process of law, of a serious infraction of law amounting to blatantly immoral conduct — the killing of a detainee after he has surrendered; the humiliation of a suspect; the molestation of a prisoner — the inevitable question is: where was his superior? Not only whether he had directly ordered the action, the subject of the trial, but whether he had promoted it, tacitly or expressly, whether he had acted to prevent it.

This is indeed a heavy burden, but it comes with and cannot be divorced from acceptance of power, of authority. There is no authority without responsibility, in every sense of that word, not only administrative and fiscal, but also — and more important — moral responsibility.

Responsibility devolves also on those who are in a position to influence the composition and the orientation of the leadership: in other words, the entire society, although not in equal measure. Here one enters a vast field in which legal norms and procedures no longer apply, but precisely because of that, moral norms should hold sway. Some time ago, in Germany, I received a pamphlet setting forth in great detail the program of events commemorating *Kristallnacht*. On every page there was the slogan: "nobody participated, nobody knew...." "Knowing nothing" of a sin committed repeatedly and with utmost publicity makes one an accessory to that sin, before or after the fact. "We are *all* to blame" — is that not the equivalent of "*no one* is guilty"? In some notable cases it has been construed in such a way. That is entirely wrong. There is a hierarchy of responsibility, of blame, of guilt, just as there is a hierarchy of punishment.

The other day I shuddered when a friend, whom I hold in the

highest esteem, told me that he turns the TV off whenever pictures
of houses being demolished on the West Bank as punishment for
terrorist acts are being shown. Whether or not this is sinful is a
subject which can and should be debated; in any case, it is being
performed in our name, on our behalf. The abdication of
responsibility may be the most sinful act of all; it is habit-form-
ing, contagious, potentially the small beginning of a long and
slippery slope.

Whoever believes that Israel was conceived in sin, that it is
nothing but the belated product of a colonial, imperialist era, of an
historical process aimed at the dispossession of Third World peoples for the benefit of the wealthy and powerful of the First and
Second Worlds, denies the legitimacy of the Jewish state and dis-
qualifies himself from pronouncing judgment on specific deeds
of that state or its emissaries. Whoever considers the very existence of Israel as an act of aggression and provocation will necessarily attribute everything that follows to that original sin and its
authors; by the same token, he absolves present-day actors from
any possible guilt. That, surely, is not the intention of those parties
to the Israel-Arab conflict, or partisans of such parties, who cling
to that view, but it is the necessary logical corollary of which they
should be aware.

By the same token, whoever declares that Israel's presence in
the Gaza Strip, Judea and Samaria (these are geographical terms,
not to be construed as ideological articles of faith) is the role of an
occupying power and lacking legitimacy will rightly be suspect
when he negatively assesses, as a rule, Israel's actions in those
territories. Those who affirm the occupation by the IDF of the West
Bank and Gaza during the Six-Day War of 1967 to be the result of a
legitimate act of self-defense, performed in the course of an unprovoked, defensive war — a "just war," in legal and moral terms
— have the right and the duty to concern themselves with the
morality of its actions there, in general, and after December 1987,
in the wake of the *intifada*, in particular.

Most legal systems include a statute of limitations whereby
what is considered as illegal at a given moment, with and because
of the passage of time, becomes if not legal, at least no longer
justiciable. I am not aware of an opposite legal or moral doctrine,
one which would convert an action, legitimate at the time it was
committed, into an illegal or immoral one with or because of the
passage of time. If, therefore, Israel's entry into and occupation of
the West Bank in 1967 was legitimate, its presence there 21 years

later must perforce be similarly considered. Anyone contesting that premise will be hard put to indicate at what precise moment the transformation from legitimacy to its negation took place.

Legitimate presence does not automatically endow with legitimacy each and every action deemed necessary to maintain that presence. The end does not sanctify *any* means. Moreover, if the pursuance of an aim, legitimate in itself, consistently or increasingly requires the adoption of measures perceived as running counter to the norms of ethical behavior, that aim in itself becomes unethical. In view of what has just been stated, the question will rightly be asked: at which precise point in time does it so become? After 10, 20, 50 years?

My answer: our presence in the West Bank as an occupying power, wielding the authority of a military government, is legitimate as long as we do not come to consider it as permanent. This may be a paradox but it is none the less true: the present situation is morally tenable as long as we do not abandon our efforts to change it; once such efforts would be unilaterally abandoned, the moral foundation of such a presence would collapse.

The permanent subjection of another people runs counter to Hillel's maxim, to Kant's categorical imperative. We ourselves do not wish to be subjected by others. This statement of principle does not accept or reject, sanctify or exclude any one of the formulas currently being bandied about in Israel's political marketplace: territorial compromise or any other form of power-sharing; permanent or temporary, partial or total solutions; direct talks or international conferences. And there may be others not yet articulated.

Jewish defense forces in Palestine, every since their inception, under Ottoman rule, the British Mandate and, since 1948, in the State of Israel have preached and, on the whole, honestly attempted to practice the doctrine which at first was known by the solemn name of *kedushat haneshek*, the sanctity of arms (which also included other elements, of no interest in the present context) and subsequently as *tohar haneshek*, the purity of arms. This does not preclude the use of arms, but severely circumscribes it. In a way it is comparable to, although not identical with, the doctrine of "proportionate and discriminate" use of force.

Its application has differed from time to time, fluctuating from the *havlaga*, the restraint of the mid-1930s which permitted only direct defense against a direct attack endangering lives (not property), to large scale punitive, retaliatory or preventive operations such as the Litani Operation of 1978 in southern Lebanon.

The doctrine differentiates between civilian and armed personnel, between active protagonists and innocent bystanders, between lethal and non-lethal weapons, between participants and supporters. Basically it is a moral yardstick, and yet, characteristically, its principal proponents have considered it expedient to provide it with hard-nosed, pragmatic, utilitarian justifications. Some were (and are) concerned about the influence of wielding disproportionate, unwarranted force on those who wield it. Young people are impressionable; it may distort their moral judgment for life.

Others, first and foremost among them Ben-Gurion, took this argument one step further: those who use force indiscriminately against Arabs, will they hesitate to do the same to Jews? It was in that spirit that Ben-Gurion in the autumn of 1948 read to the Provisional Council of State and distributed to tens of thousands of soldiers a poem by Nathan Alterman concerning the killing of innocent civilians in the town of Lydda soon after its occupation. The poet warns that soldiers and others who agree with them are in imminent danger of becoming war criminals, with slogans of "military necessity" or revenge. He proclaims that just as war itself is cruel, the application of the commandments of mercy in its conduct must be ruthless. He calls on Jewish soldiers to defend themselves against the indifference of a Jewish public which is afraid to look at itself in a mirror. The poem ends thus: "And the people's war, which has fearlessly confronted the seven armies of the Kings of the East, will not retreat from 'do not tell it in Gat'; it is not such a coward."

Still others emphasized the need of the Yishuv and subsequently the incipient Jewish state for international sympathy, for the support of public opinion which can only be won by being or appearing to be not only right in the determination of goals, but also righteous in the choice of means.

Finally there were and are those who remind us that in the long run we and the Arabs are destined to live together in this part of the world. Indiscriminate use of force may sow fear for a time, but surely it will reap hatred for much longer.

"Purity of arms," however archaic the formulation may sound in the 1980s, is still a valid guideline for military operations outside police or quasi-police actions inside the occupied territories.

Morality and Power

The differentiation between the two types of operations has caused a great deal of confusion, which has not been helped by Yasser Arafat's melodramatic declaration in Algiers before the Palestine National Council: "stone and rifle; stone and rifle" — thus, in effect, equalizing the two. Evidently, in his conception, the *intifada* inside the territories, terrorist actions outside them, and armed infiltrations from outside are part of the same struggle. This would justify the application of the same means in all three circumstances by the party which happens to be on the other side of the barricade. However, Arafat cannot be Israel's mentor and guide in this or any other area. We have to act in a manner which will enable us to look straight into the eyes of enlightened men and women, including fellow Jews, wherever they may be today, and of our children and grandchildren tomorrow.

This requires the limitation of force to the absolute minimum; the utmost care in differentiating between those guilty of illegal acts and those who are not; clear elucidation of what does and what does not constitute an illegal act; fair warning; the utmost scrupulousness in the administration of justice, including the application of legal norms and procedures at all stages of detention, investigation, adjudication and punishment.

It does not require the unconditional, unilateral abandonment of the whole or part of the West Bank and Gaza. It does not require the exposure of our citizens — Jew or Arab, or our guests from abroad — to physical danger while travelling on either side of the "green line." It does not oblige our soldiers to tolerate ridicule and provocation. It does not oblige us to stand by and watch the burning of crops and trees, factories or houses. It enables us to differentiate between stone and rifle, but does not oblige us to do so. Little David, long ago, convincingly demonstrated that a stone can be a lethal weapon.

A little boy, aged 5, was recently killed in the Gaza Strip, allegedly by a bullet fired by an Israeli soldier. A few days later an Israeli woman was burned alive, together with her three children aged 3, 2 and six months, in a bus near Jericho while travelling from Tiberias to Jerusalem. In the first case the victim was an Arab; in the second the victims were Jews. Is there a moral difference between the two?

The bus was attacked by a number of young Arabs who decided to attack a Jewish bus with firebombs. Quite obviously, for them all the passengers of such a bus were worthy targets and potential victims. The boy was killed, so it seems (the family did not permit a

80

post-mortem) by fire directed against youngsters attacking a group of soldiers. He was not an intended target; he was an innocent bystander. The general commanding the area expressed his condolences to the family; he asked other parents to keep their children away from places in which disturbances of the peace occurred. I know him well. He was sincere. I know also that there is no consolation for the bereaved family in such knowledge.

The equalization of "purity of means" with "purity of arms" has led to a perfectly understandable public debate, initially in Israel, but taken up with alacrity elsewhere, about the relative moral and legal admissibility, or otherwise, of certain types of arms: whether one type of bullet was more or less moral than another, one tear gas canister better or worse than the next. Such a debate can be and has been reduced ad absurdum. There are doubtlessly weapons which do not permit any discrimination in their application, mainly non-conventional (atomic, biological and chemical), but also of a conventional nature. However, for most others morality and legality depend upon the circumstances under which they are being used; this, incidentally, applies to tools as well as to weapons, to parts of the human body as well as to tools. Fingernails and teeth, fists and knuckles can and have been put to murderous use, so have axes and hammers, screwdrivers and knives, kitchen knives included. For someone with a military background the generalized, ill-informed debate about the relative merits of lead, plastic and rubber bullets, multiplied by the debate about permissible ranges, sounds blatantly absurd. Has the fact been considered, for instance, that one of these comes only in clusters?

This does not imply that the choice of weapons should be left entirely in the hands of professional soldiers; indeed, they would be ill-advised to undertake such an all-encompassing responsibility. It means that the civilian authority should lay down precise guidelines for conduct, and these should be publicly debated, as to how the soldiers should perform their triple, sometimes contradictory role of maintaining law and order, and protecting the civilian population in the territories; of protecting themselves; and of minimizing the application of force. Then experts should study and recommend the appropriate methods, command and control structures, and tools.

Two elements in these guidelines seem to deserve special emphasis, more than they have received by the time of this writing: consistency and warning. Even if at a given moment one tactic seems marginally preferable to another, one should think long and hard before changing; too frequent changes produce chaos, on the one hand, and fatalism, on the other. Differences in the conduct of different units, and the Arab stonethrowers have developed a sixth sense for detecting them, are to be avoided if at all possible. We all hope that the deadly game of hide and seek, stone and retreat, block and evaporate, set on fire and disappear will soon come to an end. It has cost too many lives already and each life lost makes the inevitable ultimate accommodation more difficult. But as long as it lasts, the rules of the game must be consistent; an Arab — and a Jewish — resident of Judea, Samaria and Gaza has a right to know what is and what is not permissible, and more important still, has the right to live in security and tranquility as long as he does not stray from the path.

Soon after the end of World War II, I was sent by Chaim Laskov, my company commander in the Jewish Brigade, to attend a junior leaders (roughly, platoon sergeants) course at the School of Infantry at Warminster, on the Salsbury Plains. There were the usual lessons about individual, section and platoon training and tactics, spiced with some of the lessons of the recent war. (I remember a public contest between a British Piat and an American Bazooka, both trying to hit a moving tank.) In view of the British army's current duties in what was left of the colonies, and particularly the problems it experienced in India and in Palestine, a lesson was added on the military in aid of the civilian authorities. The entire student body, some 1,000 NCOs, was assembled in the huge auditorium. On the stage was a colonial governor, typified by his cork helmet, a junior officer, and a section of soldiers. All of a sudden the rear door of the auditorium opened and in came a colorful procession in "native" garb — baggy trousers, slippers, exotic headdresses. Led by a gentleman with a red turban, soon identified by most of us as one of our sergeant instructors, they were throwing cotton balls, symbolic stones, at the authorities assembled on the stage. As soon as these realized what was happening, the governor, representing the civilian authority, through a megaphone which had been prepared in advance, warned the ominously approaching stonethrowers that their action was illegal and called on them to disperse. This was done in a strange sounding mumbo-jumbo, presumably representing Hindi or Urdu, to show that due warning — to be precise, three consecutive warnings — must be given, in a language understood by the demonstrators, in each and every event.

On Hillel, Kant and the Intifada

When the mob continued to advance, the colonial type, in writing, asked the military commander to take over and deal with the situation. The lieutenant acknowledged, in writing, the acceptance of the request. By this time the mob was close to the foot of the stage. One can imagine how much time had been spent during rehersals on the meticulous timing of this particular moment of maximum suspense. Now the officer in charge uttered the following unforgettable words, succinctly and in English: "Private Smith" (not everybody, only a totally trustworthy veteran), "one bullet" (not a machinegun burst) "at the ringleader with the red turban" (ringleaders have a moral duty to wear distinctive dress, so that Private Smith can easily identify them) "to wound and not to kill" (Private Smith, you have been warned! If your bullet will prove lethal, you, and not your superior officer, will be court-martialed). "Fire!" The sound of one (blank) bullet reverberated through the dense silence in the auditorium; the ringleader collapsed dramatically. The mob started its retreat, with the leader being carried out by his comrades. End of show, and thunderous applause.

It is not my purpose to analyze this show in detail, nor to enquire whether it was followed, or could have been followed, in practice. Nor would I dwell on the analogy between ours and a colonial situation. Israel is our metropolis, not an expendable colony. But we govern the territories, like any military government, without the consent of the governed. Their leaders have not been, nor could they be consulted. Clearly understood warnings should therefore be of double importance. What our soldiers are trained to do before opening fire is not less important than what they will do thereafter: Who should talk? And how? What kind of loudspeaking technology is employed? These are legitimate, nay vital concerns. Talking before shooting is as important in the tactical as it is in the strategic sphere.

A great deal has been said and written about media coverage of events, particularly recent events in Israel. No doubt the amount of coverage is often beyond any proportion. In Algiers, in two or three days of anti-government agitation, more people, more Arabs were killed than in almost a year of uprising in the territories. Would anyone care to compare TV footage dedicated respectively to both events? For Algiers substitute, at will: Sri Lanka\Sudan\Chad\Afghanistan\Iraq et al.

In many cases reporting was tilted, sometimes heavily tilted, toward the Arab side. Incongruously, perhaps, Arab stone-throwing youths have been depicted successively, and sometimes simultaneously, as fearless heroes twisting the tail of the Israeli lion, and as the innocent victims pounced upon by that very same lion gratuitously, without provocation on their part. An open society has to pay the price for its openness. We have no right to complain. An open society is the type of society we have striven to establish in Israel.

In such a society, the media, especially the electronic media, fulfill a vital function in conveying information to the public, on the one hand, and in formulating public opinion and conveying it to the authorities, on the other. They have tremendous power and with it commensurate responsibility. Only in a closed, autocratic society are the media above criticism. In an open society they are not entitled to immunity from scrutiny.

Theoreticians of science have long been contemplating the question as to whether absolutely objective observation and measurement of phenomena is feasible, since the very fact of being observed and measured changes the phenomena themselves. Be that as it may in the natural sciences, the answer as far as humans are concerned is clear. The fact of being observed, or rather, being aware of that fact, tends to change human conduct, as anyone who has ever watched candid camera knows.

There have been, or so it appears, some isolated cases in which impatient TV crews paid Arab youngsters to light a bonfire of car tires. They make exciting spectacles on color TV. But these cases are not the issue. In many more cases (no one can quantify responsibly), Arabs have been encouraged to take action by the very presence of TV crews. Politicians, when they are or think they are on TV, adjust their ties and repair their hairdos. Arab youngsters light tires.

This by now seems to be an accepted fact. What may be even more serious is a tendency by Israeli soldiers to adopt two different codes of conduct: one on-screen, the other off it. If that, too, becomes an established norm, TV will have outlived its usefulness as a channel for truth; it will be well on its way to becoming a distorting, ultimately corrupting influence.

During the days immediately following the Algiers declaration by the PLO, the West Bank was out of bounds for TV. During the very same days, in spite of heightened tension, there were practically no casualties reported by Israeli or Palestinian sources. Is there a causal link between the two?

To sum up: Israel's present position in Judea, Samaria and

Gaza is morally valid as long as Israel does not cease its efforts to change it. It is tenable as long as the means required for maintaining Israel's presence are compatible with the doctrine of purity of arms. It requires that all of us, soldiers and civilians, those who do their reserve duty in the casbah of Nablus and those who watch them on television at home, look at ourselves in the mirror unflinchingly and be able to live with what we see.

Israel has from the outset tacitly accepted a double standard; it has acquiesced in a situation in which one expects from Israel more than from its adversaries. Indiscriminate killing of civilians — whether Arab or Jew or, for that matter, Kurd or Yemenite, inside or outside their countries, in Hebron and Tiberias, Maalot and Jericho, Hamma and Mafraq — has for long been taken as an accepted norm where Arabs are concerned. It is not, will not and should not be accepted from Israel, first and foremost by Israelis themselves.

Experience since the beginning of the *intifada* in December 1987, with all its resultant mistakes and soul searchings, trials and errors, shows no cause to alter that determination. On the contrary, it should strengthen it.

CONSTITUTIONALISM AND CITIZEN PARTICIPATION STRENGTHEN MORAL STATECRAFT

Raquel H. Newman

As someone who has studied or been involved with the Jewish community at all levels for over 25 years as both professional consultant and volunteer, the political and social behaviors of American Jewish and Israeli Jewish relationships absorb my attention without surcease.

To my thinking, relationships between individual morality and public policy are never very clear, even though stated via media, written materials and legislation. Further, in a world of diverse and usually competing constituencies, each with agendas of self-interest, most conflict is contained in the moral behaviors of individuals and that of community through public policy. Reconciling such conflicts have been explored by political theorists for millennia and by constituted governments similarly. Neither kings, popes, dictators nor elected governments have had outstanding successes in consolidating morality among groups, individuals and whole communities.

Probably the advent of mass instant communications has exacerbated these problems. Speeches are taped, film records behavior, the jet plane transports reporters anywhere rapidly. Moral stances are diluted by the camera, by public relations, or simply by the latest piece of dramatic newsmaking. In smaller, past societies, less complex, with interactive consequences not readily connected to millions of human beings, moral choices were more limited. This is not to say these choices were less difficult in specific context. Now there is less than ten minutes warning time in which a nuclear holocaust could take place; a few hundred years ago armies needed days or months to march upon enemies. Pronouncements were occasions of drama and splendor when people gathered, ceasing ordinary labor and activity. Now, going to the beach or missing major events can be overcome by replay or recording. Thus it appears that the moral imperatives for both individuals and groups involving public policy must be valued less strongly than has been the case historically.

The famous Deuteronomic passage (Nitzavim 30:15-18) exhorts the Israelites to make the right moral choices; to do good, so that individuals and the group, with their offspring, shall live. A standard of behavior is set before tribal society that creates moral underpinnings. Public policy per se is a much later concept flowing from nation-states with a parliamentary basis, but the social and political units, even in the Hebrew Bible, show the difference between false moral behavior and acceptable stances, in the eyes of God. Thus, Moses is appalled at worship of the Golden Calf, and returns from Sinai with a Code of Law which set the stage, one may argue, for evolving public policy with a moral framework.

Behaving in a moral context has not come easily or naturally to humankind. In Genesis each patriarch exhibits severe individual moral flaws. Abraham gets ready to sacrifice his only son upon hearing God command him; Joseph steals his brother's birthright; Joseph's jealous brothers kidnap him and abandon him in a well. Plato's ideal state envisions enlightened philosopher-kings making statecraft decisions as morally precepted. However, Athenian democracy, indeed a model of citizen participation in the ancient world, flourished for roughly 50 years only and at that only a minority of the population were entitled to be cit izens. Of the world's famous rulers in the Christian era, very few rulers create morally grounded public policy to organize against social disorganization, war, or famine. The major Caesars of Rome, Constantine and Charlemagne, utilized religion as a touchstone, adding their personal charismatic stamp to provide the administrative skills or military victory that upheld public policy supporting their regimes. It is questionable whether these ruling postures can be measured in current terms for present political organizational models.

Practicing statecraft is a difficult matter, especially for new nations such as Israel. Reflecting upon the United States' experience at the end of its first 40 years, it is important to remember that gaps existed between the moral conception of becoming a nation and the execution of that mandate. Similarly so for Israel. To activate ideas of parliamentary and/or representative government requires individuals coming together, to stem larger, more compelling abuses of power and moral pressures. Only thus was King John made to sign the Magna Carta, the initial attempt by the individual nobles to challenge the moral claims to correct behavior as given by the divine right of kingship. Only after both the American and French revolutions, and in Europe following the

Treaty of Vienna in 1815, do there evolve different models of governance. The notion is that people come together for common good, morally-based enlightened self-interest, consenting to be governed. Another idea comes into play that governance needs to be good for the greatest number, not just for a privileged few, whether the designation is by reason of nobility, religion, wealth, or military power. Public policy issues show an insistence that governments must protect the individuals from not only their own interpersonal excesses, but from special interest tyrannies within government.

Within the nation-state there are multiple communities within the whole, jostling for power. Moral absolutists try to impose their psycho-social visions of public policy upon the whole, claiming right behavior. Rev. Cotton Mather tried with some successes to make Massachusetts a theocracy in the name of morality. Nazi Germany, Stalinist Russia or Mao's China each provide examples of how rigid moral absolutism, officially adopted by the state, causes dissenters or designated undesirable individuals and groups to be discredited, delegitimized and punished. Power exercised without due regard for the moral underpinning for governing in turn demoralizes or undermines the consensual basis for public policies. Choice, contest, testing and modification of governance is stifled. Protecting against excessive moralistic postures requires an elaborate set of checks and balances against the tyranny of any one small group that may weaken severely community public policy. Judicial review within the court system(s), legislative controls and administrative sanctions, together with open, free election of public officials, assist in ensuring a healthy climate for making public policy. Given the push-pull of conflicting interests of both individuals and groups within the context of governing, morality is easily compromised for power and self-interest.

During the American Civil War, President Lincoln at once held together a divided nation with moralistic entreaty while suspending the precious right of habeas corpus. Again, President Roosevelt geared up the nation to fight enemies on two fronts while illegally interning Japanese-Americans on the grounds of possible disloyalty. The moral outrage attending these behaviors did not surface immediately, nor modify public policy until long after these actions. Each president thought the acts were justified on pragmatic and moral grounds for the great good of the nation.

Presently, Israel is confronting the conflict between the self-perception of being a nation that is morally grounded and the need to act on behalf of its citizens individually and collectively as community. Yet its institutional safeguards need strengthening or revision badly. Excessively zealous individuals and small groups, claiming moral rectitude in absolute terms, are able to have undue influence. Without the equivalent of a written constitution and some sort of Bill of Rights, without directly elected representatives, without the access to alter public policy by means of initiative or referendum on the ballot, less curbs operate upon various coalition arrangements made within political parties and between the numerous parties. Public policy is readily shiftable, or conversely, hard to move. Only the courts, especially the Supreme Court, act as guardian and moral guide for conflicts in the community. Legislators need more informed decision-making skills; would there be the likes of the U.S. National Security Council or a Brookings Institution as resources.

In a very imperfect world, moral relativism is accepted, but not without question. Expectations from dictatorships are quite different than from democratic models of government. Even with a set of institutional protections referred to here, citizen vigilance is very important. Redress and discussion must flow through a free press, through open forums, and surely through the ballot box to ensure moral restraints continually against excessive or ill-founded behaviors. Both governing bodies and individuals are bound by a sense of national well-being, derived by actions that are morally responsible rather than morally right. Even if but rarely do individual morality and public policy coincide well, pursuit of such goals is necessary. That meshing may express itself during times of crises, but the daily business of governing is most healthy when statecraft can use its own checks and balances for the nation's psychological and social growth against natural pressures, to achieve collective self-interest.

THE MATTER OF MORALITY AND ISRAELI FOREIGN POLICY

Earl Raab

In some American Jewish circles, it has become common to attack Israel's foreign policy as violative of moral standards, unseemly for a Jewish state. That alleged breach of morality, applied to the Lebanese invasion, has most notably been applied to Israel's treatment of the Palestinians in the West Bank and Gaza.

It is customary to attack this notion by pointing out that it makes no distinction between governmental and individual imperatives. As George F. Kennan once put it, government's "primary obligation is to the *interests* of the national society it represents, not to the moral impulses that individual elements of the society may experience." Those interests, as far as foreign policy are concerned, have to do mainly with national security. However, that distinction begs the question for Jewish critics, who often point out that Israel is a Jewish state and therefore inherently required to conduct itself according to "Jewish values." But that way lies an unending morass of debate as to the nature of Jewish values. There are those who learnedly hold that the Jewish values of a Jewish state biblically mandate more extensive boundaries; and others who learnedly hold that Jewish values require Israel not to be a state at all.

When the modern-day critics of a too harsh Israeli foreign policy invoke the Jewish values of a Jewish state, they are obviously referring to certain selected Jewish values, usually of the prophetic persuasion. The selectivity of those values does not diminish them, but it does move the discussion to another point.

In short, those selected "Jewish values" are values which those critics feel should apply to any enlightened state, Jewish or not, even though these critics might have more of an emotional investment in the actions of Israel. The question of state morality is less murkily — and more honestly — handled by defining Israel, for this purpose, as a Jewish state because the great majority of its citizens are Jewish, and because Israel has been and is a treasured homeland and refuge for Jews from around the often hostile world. It is in that light at least that the moral aspects of Israeli foreign policy can best be examined. Certainly there are moral strictures which apply, but they are essentially the same that should apply to all states.

On this plane, the usual distinction is made between the consequential, sometimes called the utilitarian, and the absolutist approaches to morality. One, of course, is primarily concerned with the consequences of an act; while the absolutist is primarily concerned with the act itself. No blueprint ensues for most people from this distinction, but it does set up some parameters for a reasonable discussion.

After the recent Israeli election, a spokesman for Shas (the Sephardic Torah Guardians — an ultra-Orthodox political party), invoking the Jewish values of *halakhah,* said: "If it can prevent the death of one Jew to return the territories, they will be returned. But not if it will cause the death of two others."

That is a permutation of consequential morality. As for the exclusivity of his reference to Jewish lives, that is a reflection of wartime morality, wherein the primary responsibility of a state is to the lives of its own citizens. When the United States dropped the atomic bomb on Hiroshima, the announced equation was that the lives of tens of thousands of American servicemen were thereby saved.

Almost all of us operate within some form of consequential morality — and especially states do so, by charge. But the modern world would probably not be operable with either a "pure" utilitarianism or a "pure" absolutism on this score — although there are advocates of feckless relativism, on the one hand, and of rigid absolutism, on the other. For most people and for most states, in their different fashions, there are "absolute" values which limit consequential morality, and consequential morality is itself some judgmental balance of "absolute" values.

It is thus part of an enlightened utilitarianism that every human life is precious and not to be violated wantonly, without dire necessity. That, of course, applies not just to killing, but to the imposition of any seriously oppressive or demeaning life circumstances. It also applies to the life of the actor.

The most enlightened state is the one required to make judgment calls most excruciating at times of threat or duress. The judgment calls are about consequences, not about the isolated "absolute" values which limit their consideration. The government of a humanitarian Abraham Lincoln doggedly pursued the extremely bloody Civil War, if not to end slavery, then to forestall the perceived human consequences of a split Union.

As far as the morality of a state is concerned, the anarchic excesses of that or any war only requires the state to react with credible insistence on the limiting absolute values. When General Grant ordered all Jewish traders removed from the war zones — as a bigoted military measure against illegal cotton-trading (Grant's pique was especially aroused when Grant's own father became involved in such illegal trading) — Lincoln immediately reversed the general's action.

Many judgments hold that World War I was an immoral war in itself, frivolously squandering lives without any moral purpose. No credible judgment holds that World War II as waged by the Allies was an immoral war in itself, given the probably human consequences if it were not waged. That was a clear judgment of utilitarian morality. But it is a matter of moral controversy whether, within that judgment, the saturation bombing of Dresden, presumably killing masses of civilians in order to make a persuasive point, exceeded the bounds of necessity and of limiting human values. Truman's Hiroshima decision has similarly caused controversy in some quarters. Even wartime morality, at its best, has some limiting concern with unnecessarily taking enemy lives, even though the first consideration is with friendly lives.

Senator Eugene McCarthy, a leader of the opposition to the Vietnam War, once said that the war had become immoral at the point when it became clear that the U.S. could not win it — and persevered nonetheless, with great loss of life on both sides. That is another example of consequential morality. But within that context, the My Lai massacre by some American soldiers was considered by the state an immoral act in itself because its wanton violation of life went beyond the bounds of necessity.

Another example of the problematics of consequential morality as applied to foreign policy has to do with the matter of a state making allies with another state whose values with respect to human life and human rights are, at the least, suspect. Franklin D. Roosevelt was in utilitarian voice when he said of a South American dictator, "He is a son of a bitch, but he is our son of a bitch." That was not necessarily a "cynical" expression. It is, of course, a prime utilitarian function of the state to maintain national security. But there are, at best, some countervailing "absolute" values.

To put it another way, it is a matter of risks. A "moral" society, whose explicit values include the preciousness of human life and freedom, should subject itself to great risks before breaching those values. A simple example is the precept that it is better to conduct a judicial system so that ten guilty criminals will go free rather than one innocent person be jailed.

There are a thousand examples of such civilized risk-taking. According to the Geneva Conventions of War, it is forbidden to kill prisoners who attempt to escape, even though they may some-day succeed and end up in an opposing army. It is forbidden to torture prisoners in order to extract information, even though the lack of that information may conceivably put friendly lives at risk.

But, alas, even such proscriptions are more limiting than absolute. A given individual's conscience may dictate that he will take the ultimate risk under any circumstances, that he will not kill even though it seems almost certain that he will himself be killed otherwise. But we cannot morally make that choice when it comes to risking other lives. That is what "national security" is finally about; the state is charged at best with protecting the lives and freedom of its citizens. At its moral best, it must maximize its risk-taking for the sake of other values, but not finally abandon its charge.

Thus, circumstances alter the consequential equation. The moral brink changes for different states under different conditions. A powerful and invulnerable state, even under duress, can afford to take almost any risk in order to keep its moral skirts clean. Not so a relatively weak and vulnerable state. The moral imperative for both is to be bounded by the "absolute" values up to but not beyond sheer survival. That is finally a consequential measurement itself, a balancing act, although the "absolute" human values give us our points of measurement.

If the failure of a state to survive means a genocidal threat to the lives of the population, or even its virtual enslavement, then consequential measurement seems more clear-cut. However, if the failure of a state to survive means primarily the end of a political system, a life-style, even an autonomy, then the moral worthiness of that state, political system, and life-style must enter into the consequential equation, as assessed by some "absolute" values.

When Franklin D. Roosevelt referred favorably to a dictator as "our son of a bitch," the hub of his highest and consequential concern was presumably a world system which would best guarantee the survival of the American state and society. By a preponderance of absolute moral values which are admittedly judgmental, the survival of the American state and society is worthy and even important for the world.

With all its serious but remediable flaws, the United States is the standard-bearer of certain fundamental values of political freedom and democracy which have altered the world — even recently, the communist world. But even if it were not important for the world, the survival of the American state would be a morally worthy goal for its own citizenry. Its failure to survive as a result of outside intervention — as well as by internal subversion — would be morally disastrous.

By contrast, a morally bankrupt state has little or no capital with which to invoke validity for its actions for survival. A relativism which would say that Hitler's Reich had some moral mandate to survive because it was chosen by a majority of the population or because it had some cultural authenticity must simply be denied by moral fiat.

But even here, in the world as it exists, a consequential logic must be applied in many cases. The "our-son-of-a-bitch" syndrome can be morally valid if the cause is just enough, if the risk-taking is high enough, if the unsavory partnership is necessary enough. A classic example was the American and Western alliance with the state which, at the time, had murdered certainly millions of its citizens, literally enslaved millions more, and was by statistical count history's most massive violator of human rights. That was the Soviet Union of the 1940s with whom the United States and the West made firm alliance in the war against Nazi Germany, a more qualitative threat to the values of Western democracy. Consequential morality is revealed as lesser-evil morality.

It is clear to me that the survival of the State of Israel is not only morally worthy but imperative. The internal decency of the state, all religious controversies and political flaws notwithstanding, sustain that judgment.

Furthermore, the failure of the State of Israel to survive would, beyond most other cases, mean a direct and palpable threat to the physical lives of many of its citizens, and to the freedom of the survivors. The moral consequences would be predictably calamitous. Israel is also a highly vulnerable state, with relatively little room for risk-taking.

It is within that set of consequences that the absolute moral values play out. When it is said that morally valid states take risks in order to maintain their moral character, the statement means something circumstantially different for Israel than it means for the United States, or even for Egypt.

Indeed, with that understanding, moral assessment of Israeli foreign policy takes on the highest level of difficulty, not because immoral options are more justified, but because so many inherently moral actions are consequentially balanced.

Wanton, vengeful, excessive punitive policies against individuals or groups are certainly censurable, although sometimes difficult to assess. But the moral critics of Israel are really and sensibly more interested in attacking policies which *result* in acts of oppression of and violence against Palestinian Arabs. Thus, the most serious charges of immorality are variously directed against such Israeli behavior as: refusing self-determination for the Palestinians, refusing to negotiate with the PLO, refusing generally to accommodate enough in the cause of peace, attempting to maintain control over the territories, attempting to maintain order in the territories.

Insofar as these negative policies are promulgated and supported for venal or imperialistic reasons, then there is standing for the case of "immorality," given the human consequences of these policies. But — exceptions noted — the vast majority of Israelis who support such policies do so for moral reasons, out of their own formulations of consequential morality. The mainstream elements of the Israeli government do the same.

The differences that severely split the Israeli populace — and, to a lesser extent, the American Jewish populace — are for the most part not moral in nature, but simply strategic. Under the difficult circumstances that obtain, what is the best practical course towards the accomplishment of the highest human values, peace, and the least possible violation of others without endangering survival? That is what most of the differences are about.

There is no need to rehearse the strategic differences, ranging from the relatively hard-line approach which points out that Sadat came to Israel when Begin's strategy reigned (and Gorbachov came to disarmament when Reagan's strategy reigned), to the relatively flexible approach which suggests that the current objective situation, different than that of the Begin era, can only deteriorate to the catastrophic disadvantage of Israel and peace, and therefore strategically requires a guarded initiative from Israel.

Many of the latter strategists also believe that a continuation of the status quo, under the circumstances, aside from corroding the democratic nature of Israel, will harden inter-ethnic hatreds and fears to the point where any reasonable strategic debate will be corrupted, and peace will be made increasingly difficult.

The strategic debate is crucial. But many Israelis and most American Jews are too paralyzed by fear and by the cross-winds of that debate to fruitfully engage in it. Broadsiding inappropriate charges of "immorality" can only feed that paralysis and generally confuse the debate. Conversely, avoiding the "moral" argument where it is inappropriate need not tame the debate. A given strategy need not be particularly "immoral" by any standard in order to be mistaken, ill-conceived, or even stupid.

THE MORALITY OF ACTS IS DETERMINED BY THE ENDS THEY SERVE

Emanuel Rackman

The legal philosopher Rudolph Stammler held that there could be such a thing as natural law with a variable content. For me, there are moral absolutes as ideals but in practice the morality of a specific act is determined by the end it purports to serve. Nothing is evil except by reference to its goal. If in order to achieve a worthy objective we refuse to adopt a course which is evil, it is not because we are avoiding the evil means but rather because we want to serve still another end which ranks higher than the end for which we are considering the allegedly evil means.

This can be illustrated from the writings of two philosophers — one non-Jewish and the other Jewish. The former is identified with villainy of the first order; the latter, with saintliness of the highest degree. They are Machiavelli, on the one hand, and Bachya ibn Pakuda, on the other.

In the history of political thought Machiavelli is regarded as the exponent of the notion that sovereigns may do anything — steal, murder, cheat and betray — in order to keep themselves in power. He is, therefore, often called the prophet of immorality — or amorality. However, this is not true. Machiavelli simply held that there were two ends that ranked higher than all other ends. These are the life and liberty of the state. Since there are no ends worthier than these, when these ends must be served one cannot be deterred by considerations of justice or injustice, humanity or cruelty, glory or shame. If Machiavelli had maintained that the life of an individual is as important as the life of the state, a position very much supported by the *halakhah*, he might not have urged his Prince to be so "knife-happy" or "poison-happy." One must take issue with him not as to whether the use of foul means is proper or improper, but rather as to what are the highest ends. For that reason the philosophy of *halakhah* is so much sounder.

Halakhic discussions are always with respect to ends. One asks: "Which end, which *mitzvah*, ranks higher, so that a lesser one gives way or is altogether disregarded?" We do not speak of ends justifying or not justifying means. Every deed and every thing serves some end. Even our involuntary breathing is related to an end — the *mitzvah* of self-preservation. This end, however, may yield in one case to a higher end — as in the case of martyrdom for the sanctification of God's name — or it may not yield to that end as in the many instances when it is permitted to violate the law and save one's life.

Bachya makes this clear in a passage of his *Duties of the Heart* in connection with that incident in Samuel's life when God told him to lie to Saul in order to save his life (I Samuel 16:2). When Samuel hesitated to go to Saul lest Saul kill him, God did not tell him to place his trust in the Lord; instead, He directed him to use a subterfuge. Thereby, says Bachya, God gave His approval to the abuse of truth in self-defense, even though He could have admonished the prophet for his lack of faith in Him who has the ultimate power of life and death over all of us.

The pursuit of truth is also a *mitzvah*. Nonetheless, there are other *mitzvot* to which it yields. In a similar vein one might interpret the two dissimilar prohibitions on the Torah not to lie. In Exodus the command is to keep one's distance from falsehood. In Leviticus the command is simply not to lie. It appears from numorous commontators that tho Lovitical command is a relative one; it yields in the interest of domestic peace. God Himself lied to Abraham when He reported to the husband about Sarah's statement that her husband was old. In Exodus, on the other hand, the command is part of a code pertaining to courts of law. In courts of law there can be no compromise with truth. Witnesses must not conceal or doctor their testimony, no matter what the consequences.

The Torah's interest in justice is an interest so high in the hierarchy of interests that it would be defeated if witnesses could take liberties and revise their stories in the interest of good will or domestic tranquility. To such an extent is unequivocal, absolute truth the desideratum in a court of justice that the ingenious author of the *Meshech Hochmah* explains that the reference in the ninth commandment of the Decalogue is to a false witness, and not to false testimony, because even if what the witness is telling is the truth, but the witness knows the truth only by hearsay and not because he saw the facts, he is a false witness: the testimony itself may be true, but the witness is a liar, for he is making himself appear as a competent witness when he is not.

Thus the *halakhah* never approved of the extreme attributed to Immanuel Kant that one may never lie. There are times even in a court of law, for example, when the obligation to tell the truth may be suspended — when the court of law is not one in which justice is really meted out. Indeed, there is one responsum among the many written by R. Meir of Rothenburg to the effect that a Jew may not tell the truth in a non-Jewish court which is given to the persecution of Jews, when, thereby, damage would result to a co-religionist. For telling the truth, the Jew in such a case is held accountable to the aggrieved party; his obligation is to lie.

Professors Dewey and Tufts in their textbook on *Ethics* define moral experience as "that kind of conduct in which there are ends so discrepant, so incompatible, as to require selection of one and rejection of the other....It is incompatibility of ends which necessitates consideration of the true worth of a given end; and such consideration it is which brings the experience into the moral sphere."

Thus, almost every time that a Jew exercises free will — *behirah* — with regard to his performance of an overt act, he is having a moral experience. He is choosing between incompatible ends. Sometimes the ends are incompatible because one is God-given and the other Satan-inspired. Sometimes both ends are God-given, and the choice is dictated by *halakhah*. Sometimes the ends are God-given, and the *halakhah* enjoins one to make one's own choice.

This brings us to a further point. Does the *halakhah* ever bid one to exercise one's own moral consciousness to ignore one of its own norms because of an end also *halakhically* approved but for which there is no special rule calling for its possible violation — unlike the case of a positive commandment which is to be obeyed even if it involves a violation of a prohibition? There is authority for an affirmative answer.

Two such general instances are known to the *halakhah*. The first is based on the verse "When the time has come to act for the Lord, they violate Thy Torah." True, the authority given in this verse is dangerously broad. One should never exercise it without the greatest caution. However, the two historic instances cited in Talmud when this authority was exercised are revealing. Rashi cites Elijah's sacrifice outside of Jerusalem on Mt. Carmel as a biblical precedent. But this instance could have been a *hora'at sha'ah*, a crisis or emergency decision. The two historic instances were: First, to permit the use of God's name when we greet one another; for the end of peace — for the end of brotherhood — we violate the commandment in the Decalogue not to make needless mention of the Creator. Second, to permit the writing of the Oral Law, or

more correctly as Prof. Czernowitz interprets the matter, to permit
the use of written materials to teach the Oral Law. If this permis-
sion had not been granted, who knows whether Judaism would
have survived except among a handful in every generation. The
revolutionary character of this decision can only be fathomed in
the light of the text that compares one who commits *halakhic*
precedents to writing to one who burns the Torah (B.T. *Temurah*
14b)! Nonetheless, the final ruling was that one may commit the
Oral Law to writing.

II

With this as background one can only answer the questions
raised in this symposium by reference to specific situations. The
specific situation will make a difference between what is moral
for the individual and what is moral in public policy. For example, I may dislike much about my neighbor's behavior in home
and on his grounds, in his personal appearance, how he talks to
his children, etc., but it would be immoral for me to annoy him or
to be a nuisance to him because of any dislike. If the condition so
deteriorates that I can no longer suffer the situation, then I may
have to consider changing my residence but not hurt him. Yet, a
state or one of its subdivisions is not immoral if it curbs in its
midst behavior by residents which is objectionable to the majority
provided that there is a reasonable basis for their complaints.

Moreover, within a state, an organized political community, a
corporation or an unincorporated association may have interests
which conflict with the interests of other similar groups and for
that reason may be considered selfish and immoral but the state
may prefer to permit the immoral deeds in order to serve the important cause of freedom of association or pluralism. The constituents of each of the groups may then continue to deem the pro-
motion of their particular interests as moral because they serve
still another end, e.g., the preservation of ethnic and religious
identity for ideological reasons.

In times of crisis, states may have no alternative but to act in
such a way that in normal times would be considered immoral.
During World War II the United States, for example, did that vis-
a-vis its native born citizens of Japanese origin. Israel in the *intifada* is very much in the same situation.

If it is moral to resist one who threatens your life then it is equally moral for states to do so. But as the right to self-defense is limited to means that are necessary to frustrate the attacker, so states must try to do no more than the removal of the threat requires. It is in this connection that the army or the police of the State of Israel may be faulted, but the burden of proof will be on those who accuse. When one acts in self-defense, the measure of force required to save oneself is not the same as when one is not acting under duress.

If one wants to be critical of Machiavelli then one might argue that the life of the state may be a moral end — but not its liberty. If the enemy wants only to subordinate and colonialize the threatened state, perhaps the morality of Epictetus is a higher morality. In other words, one should prefer to act morally and avoid war, even if it means the loss of national freedom, than to resort to all the "immoral" approaches that Machiavelli suggests to preserve the state's freedom. Israel is not even given this option in her present crisis. The enemy's threat is not simply to conquer but to conquer and destroy.

Consequently, the only basis for faulting Israel in her present crisis is to prove that she is exercising too much force. However, when one proves this in the case of certain individuals in the states' service, Israel has been speedy in prosecuting the offenders. Yet even in this connection one must bear in mind the measure of the rebel's provocation.

III

Thus far I have dealt only with the morality of Israel's stance. However, what is the moral situation from the point of view of those who look upon the State of Israel as an illegitimate entity that is not entitled to loyalty or obedience? One need not spell out the details — the position of many of them is clear — they are resisting invaders in nothing less than a war against piracy.

If such be their stance then they must realize that what they are doing does not enjoy the status of a lawful war by the prevailing law of nations. Israel is a state recognized (in the legal sense of the term) by the nations of the earth. Therefore, the legal status of those who want to destroy her is no better than that of outlaws. They could resist passively but for their violence they can be exiled or executed.

There are also many who do not take the extreme PLO position that Israel is to be denied recognition. They accept the existence of Israel as irreversible but they deem Israel as the conqueror and occupier of certain parts of the country. They too may engage in passive resistance because they are unhappy with the occupation. But for resort to violence there is no legal or moral warrant. Professor Emil Fackenheim deems violent action by them a withdrawal from the "social contract." And if they engage in violent action they must account for it. One may empathize with them because of the miserable situation in which they find themselves. And one may fault Israel for not having done enough to ameliorate their condition. Unfortunately there is a limit as to how much Israel can do even if the rest of the world would permit her to do so. Yet the violence is costly to the victims from the point of view of life and limb even more than to others and it is also counterproductive from the point of view of the end sought.

There are means to protest lawfully and only these should be used. Already the *intifada* has sowed seeds of hate not only in Palestinians, but in the hearts of those who never knew hate before — hundreds of thousands of Israelis.

Call it what one will — the present war may bring no good whatever. It will serve no end other than to afford a release from exasperation. There is no moral basis for it and so it should be understood.

"A LIGHT UNTO THE NATIONS"

Ismar Schorsch

Israel embodies a unique historical achievement, which remains undimmed after forty years: namely, the reversal of two millennia of national homelessness. The recovery of political sovereignty in the very land in which it was lost to the Romans in the year 62 BCE is a singular expression of unbroken historical consciousness steeled by religious faith. What is more, Israel's sterling record of commitment to democracy, political stability, absorption of refugees, social equity, agricultural development, scientific excellence, cultural creativity, and military prowess, compiled under the most adverse of conditions, is unmatched by any other state founded after the Second World War.

Israel also represents the most potent force for Jewish unity in a secular age in which the Jewish people has become deeply fragmented religiously. Israel stirs the emotions of secular and religious Jews alike, especially in moments of crisis. Its very existence, according to Abraham Joshua Heschel, helped alleviate the anguish of the Holocaust, and its stunning accomplishments inspired diaspora Jews with awe, pride, and ethnic commitment.

The pervasive political ethos of modern Jewry since the emancipation has been democratic and not authoritarian for very good reason. The extension of varying degrees of equality of Jews in countries like England, France, Prussia and Russia was always related to a broader revolutionary thrust to restructure the body politic, and hence the advocates of Jewish emancipation were never to be found among the defenders of the old order. Not surprisingly, Jews aligned themselves with the politics of their benefactors and embraced the vision of a free society based on the rule of law. Whatever their individual preference today, Jews in the diaspora remain viscerally committed to the political culture of Western democracy.

The rising tide of contempt for this political culture in Israel among certain right wing circles and all too many young people threatens the basic accord on this issue that has existed between Israel and the diaspora since the founding of the state, especially if Meir Kahane and his ilk are saying what others merely think.

Jews cannot denounce Le Pen in France and back Kahane in Israel. Such blatant hypocrisy would not only repel diaspora Jewry but mock the founders of Israel itself. To trifle with Israel's commitment to democracy is a faustian gamble that will cost all Jews dearly.

The *intifada* erupted during the Zionist Congress in December and has yet to be quelled. Despite the merciless scrutiny of the media, it has been handled with a degree of restraint reminiscent of the Haganah's policy of *havlagah* (self-restraint) toward the Palestinian uprisings of the 1930s, and surely with less brutality and bloodshed than usually mark the repression of a national rebellion. Still, the eruption is deeply troubling. The matter is far too important to all Jews to remain silent. Israel's fate hangs in the balance, and we should not be cowed by voices of authority and expertise. Well-informed judgment is a good instrument for seeing the obvious.

What is obvious after ten months of insurrection is that the struggle has finally come down to one between the actual inhabitants of the land, the Israelis and the Palestinians. The surrounding Arab states which had led the battle against Israel since 1948 have withdrawn from the fray. Egypt settled for a separate peace after a semblance of victory in the Yom Kippur War to which it has adhered despite much Israeli intransigence and provocation. Jordan has maintained a peaceful border with Israel at least since 1970 when it drove out the PLO. Israel's invasion of Lebanon proved that Syria will not fight alone, and there is little prospect of a quick rapprochement between Syria and Iraq, regardless of what happens between Iraq and Iran. If anything, it is probably that reduction of tensions in the region and the continued impotence of the PLO that eventually drove the Palestinians in desperation to seize the initiative.

In short, Israel is confronted with an internal and not an external problem. A population of one-and-a-half million Palestinians in Gaza and on the West Bank has made it poignantly clear that it will no longer suffer Israeli rule, whatever its material benefits. Forty-one years after the original UN plan to partition the country, the idea is finally gaining acceptance among a growing number of Palestinians, and that long-retarded step forward offers a glimmer of hope for a political settlement between the only two parties directly affected by the creation of Israel. The *intifada* has not challenged Israel's security as much as its moral fiber. To paraphrase the biting comment of the late and beloved Ernst Simon, the Palestine problem has become an internal Jewish problem in much the same manner as anti-Semitism is essentially an internal Christian problem.

However, a willingness to trade land for peace is anathema to the romantic, messianic mindset of the national camp in Israel. The stunning victory of 1967 blunted the pragmatic spirit which had built Israel and unleashed a fervor of messianic triumphalism which eventually transvalued Judaism itself. The settlement of Judea and Samaria and even Gaza suddenly loomed as a supreme commandment. Joshua superseded Moses and his book of conquests that of the *Humash*. The Arab became Amalek reincarnate and the much touted stranger of the Bible redefined as a convert to Judaism. To this potent mix, Menachem Begin added the bitter resentment still seething from the trauma of the Holocaust. It was now foisted as a worldview and a basis for foreign policy. As the popular song of the 1970s put it: *"ha-olam kulo negdeinu* (the whole world is against us)."

The consequences of this mindset have been nothing short of catastrophic — a misguided venture into Lebanon, a government held hostage by extremists on the West Bank, the privatization of arms, the brutalization of Israel's youth and a refusal to address the Palestinian problem.

In 1971 in an essay entitled "Education for Humanity in Time of War," Yigal Alon wrote: "If we shall be a light unto ourselves, perhaps we will also be a light unto others. Certainly not before." The Judaism of the West Bank, of Gush Emunim, is without light. The basest form of modern nationalism in Jewish garb, it violates the most fundamental of biblical injunctions: "You shall not copy the practices of the land of Egypt where you dwelt, or of the land of Canaan to which I am taking you; nor shall you follow their customs" (Lev. 18:3). The Judaism I know cares deeply for the welfare of mankind. The book of Genesis is not only about the promise of the Land but also its purpose. Abraham and his descendants were called by God to be a source of universal blessing, a model of virtue to counter the lure of paganism. And the land was to be a laboratory for a noble experiment: the formation of a just and righteous society. But the vision had first to be limned in blood. Suffering would intensify the passion for justice. After his victory over the four kings, Abraham the warrior could have seized the land immediately, but the experience of oppression and slavery had to precede the achievement of statehood. The Bible's ubiquitous compassion for the stranger, the non-Israelite, is rooted in the degradation of Egyptian bondage.

Nor was the land ever granted unconditionally. On the contrary, its retention came to be regarded as a function of the piety and justice of its body politic. To pervert God's law would defile the land and lead to expulsion. The world harbored enough decadent societies. The language of the Bible is visceral. "So let not the land spew you out for defiling it, as it spewed out the nation that came before you" (Lev. 18:28). God's impatience with Israel throughout the Bible is a measure of the universal stakes. Mankind needs a mentor. After the failure of the flood to alter human nature, God took recourse to instruction by example. Israel's waywardness imperils the very survival of the human race.

Jewry's long exilic ordeal deepened the message of its mission. Outside their homeland, they once again became the proverbial stranger of the biblical text. The manner of their treatment would measure the humanity of the nation in which they lived. The recurring struggle by Jews the world over to maintain their distinctive faith and communal autonomy delivered an implicit claim for the existence of an inalienable right to be different. From the Roman Empire to interwar Europe, Jews sought legal protection for their religious and cultural independence. The cumulative weight of their endurance and success legitimized the value and beauty of diversity. In the picturesque words of Moses Mendelssohn to Christian Europe: "Dear brother, you are well-meaning. But do not let yourselves be deceived! To belong to this omnipresent shepherd, it is not necessary for the entire flock to graze in one pasture or to enter and leave the master's house through just one door."

Zionism did not triumph by betraying that noble religious and historical legacy. The restoration of Zion would create, as Alon put it, "a model of totally moral Jewish existence in a model human society." The parochialism of Judaism always had at its core an ecumenical thrust. Our exercise of power must continue to accord with the lofty moral standards we espoused when powerless, for that is the ultimate biblical sanction of a Jewish state — to validate our vision in the crucible of reality.

MORALITY AND PUBLIC POLICY

Meir Sheetrit

While both the individual and the state find themselves in moral quandaries, the state must cope with such a predicament more frequently, given the range and scope of a modern state's involvements. The moral cost of an action may be paid both at the moment of decision or at a future date. Israel in 1984 consented to the release of over a thousand convicted terrorists, including those involved in the massacre of civilians. The decision was taken on the basis of two potent moral imperatives: the age-old Jewish concept of ransoming captives as well as the modern state's obligation to assure the security of those who serve in the armed forces. Nonetheless it was apparent at the time of the decision that the exchange would provide a boost to terrorism. Since many of the released terrorists were allowed to return to areas under Israeli control they were lionized by Arabs and appeared to corroborate the impression that Israeli resolve was crumbling.

We are paying part of the price during the *intifada*. Some of the former detainees are actively participating and orchestrating the events; others have been encouraged by the deterioration of Israel's deterrent capability. The problem of conflicting moral imperatives is not Israel's alone and falls even more heavily on the superpowers. During the twilight of the Shah's rule in Iran, the Iranian regime was under pressure from the American government not to unleash the army against the Khomeini-inspired mobs. It is at least arguable that a use of force by the Iranian army, which would have drawn the fiery condemnations of the moralists, would have spared the Iranian people a great deal of suffering. Those who counseled the United States to abandon Vietnam and "stop the bloodshed" on moralistic grounds must contend with the obvious fact that suffering and bloodshed in southeast Asia including the atrocities of the Khmer Rouge intensified as a result of the American abandonment of the region.

No one can contend that we are dealing with easy decisions but it is a national government's responsibility to confront them, not to avoid confrontation with them. The quest for an absolutely unimpeachable moral position is a trap which usually redounds to the advantage of the amoral.

The American isolationist position on the eve of the Second World War rested on the "plague on both your houses" assumption. As both Nazi Germany and the Allies were at fault, America should not sully its hands by involvement in the conflict. The attempt to justify inaction against the aggressor produced a microscopic inspection of the faults of his intended victim. This concept of morality effectively harks back to the New Testament concept that only people without sin are entitled to cast the first stone. Action is permissible only when it is performed by the morally perfect. Since very few qualify, the admonition is tantamount to endorsing passivity. Alternatively it leads those who wish to avoid moral qualms to search for amoral surrogates who can perform the distasteful tasks.

In the early stages of the uprising, some Israeli politicians yearned for King Hussein to assume the burden of controlling the territories. With Hussein in charge, they argued, there would be no further incidence of stone-throwing. These politicians did not pretend that it was Hussein's moral leadership which would deter stone-throwing, they relied on his lack of moral qualms and full attention to raison d'etat. The Jewish retort to this moralistic stance is perhaps contained in the Rabbinic aphorism: "Jephtah in his generation carries the same weight as Samuel in his generation." The biblical description of Jephtah and his associates as well as the tragic fate of Jephtah's daughter hardly certify Jephtah as a paragon of virtue. Yet it is Jephtah who eloquently defends the morality of Israelite policy in the pre-war diplomatic skirmishing with Amon. Morality therefore is not just for the official scorer on the sidelines but for the protagonists as well, even if the protagonist is partially blemished. Morality is enhanced by engagement and not by abdication.

I remain skeptical regarding the institutional steps that governments can take to minimize immorality. The educational system of any country should inculcate moral values. A pluralist democracy will have institutions such as the media, the synagogue or church, the academic world, etc. which should have the freedom to raise their voices in the event of intolerable acts. To go further than that and set up some moral government watchdog will not assist the problem; it may compound it. There will be a tendency to focus on the immediate and surface moral issues and ignore their consequences. To recur to Hans Morgenthau's introduction to *International Politics*, Neville Chamberlain very well may have been a far more moral person than Winston Churchill but Churchill proved himself better at repelling the ultimate onslaught of barbarism.

Former President Carter's and Ambassador Andrew Young's moralistic bent was evident, but it is questionable as to whether they advanced global morality because of it.

It is hard to come down firmly for either a morally relativist or absolute position. What many Israelis resent is a dual system of accounting which obtains the worst of both worlds. By the time that this article is published, the PLO will have convened in the very same Algiers where Shazli Ben Jedid's troops mowed down more civilians in one week than all the civilian fatalities that occurred in the *intifada*. No unambiguous condemnation has been issued with regard to the Iraqi use of chemical and biological warfare against both the Iranians and the Kurds.

The stock answer is that Israel should be flattered by its membership in some sort of moral major league and the responsibilities which this membership confers, while the actions of the moral miscreants are concomitant with the minor league or bush league morality to which they have been assigned. This consolation would be convincing if the violators of international morality were assigned a pariah status. This argument would also be tenable if there was no interaction between the bearers of the two standards of morality. We instead confront a situation in which the demands of morality are pressed most vigorously on the moral while the amoral are written off at the very outset.

Since a large degree of interaction does exist, the moral are placed at a disadvantage. No outcry is raised when during the *intifada* so-called collaborators are stabbed and chopped to death, or lynched, when enterprises which refuse to adhere to the dictates of the strike committees are burned, but Israelis are expected to exercise restraint and play according to the Marquis of Queensberry rules. What has generally obtained in international politics is either a moral Gresham's Law of base morality driving out the nobler or ironically, a situation where the threat of total immorality maintains some modicum of civility.

Germany, which employed poison gas in World War I, refrained from using it militarily in World War II since it knew that Britain would use poison gas in return. Similarly the concept of mutually assured destruction which dominates deterrence theory relies on the threat of indiscriminate annihilation to ensure stability. International society functions best if all parties adhere to morality; it can somehow be sustained by the knowledge that no side has a monopoly on immorality. It will founder if the wicked are allowed to prosper in their immorality while the moral are occasionally awarded merit badges amidst demands for a display of yet more fastidious moral virtue. It must be admitted that this double standard has been partially self-imposed.

There has been an historic tendency among Jews to exculpate Arabs on the ground that they were primitive and child-like or were held in the grips of feudal or irresponsible leaders. The Arabs have perennially been assigned the status of minors who could not be held accountable for their actions. It is therefore incomprehensible why the Arabs should be allowed to demand as an opener a return to previous boundaries which they attempted to erase in unsuccessful wars of annihilation against Israel.

We have been justly traumatized by the bestial policies of regimes on the right and left who have justified their crimes in the name of lofty goals, and we dutifully recite that the ends do not always justify the means. Unfortunately this statement has been internalized to the point that we have ceased altogether to examine the merits of certain ends. We no longer ponder the question of whether the means are proportional to the ends or what necessitated the employment of these means. Instead we embrace the image fostered by a visceral (and selective) media sensationalism hook, line and sinker. Nothing is worthwhile if we have to perform distasteful actions. This predicament has accompanied the Zionist movement from the onset. Zeev Jabotinsky observed the dismay in some quarters of the Zionist movement as the realization dawned that Arab opposition to a Jewish Homeland would necessitate a recourse to force.

An historical truth, Jabotinsky noted then, is not invalidated by the occasional need to employ distasteful means. The historical truth of the Zionist movement is still valid. The means employed have not been disproportionate by any international standard and they have not been means of Israel's choosing. Perhaps the other contributors will be able to supply some moral angst: I cannot do so.

PURSUING PEACE IN THE MIDDLE EAST

Max Singer

Israel is likely to survive if Israelis are united in support of the country. And Israeli is in serious danger if the deep divisions among Israelis continue and worsen. That is, Israel's safety depends on the unity of Israelis. The unity upon which Israel's survival depends, depends in turn on the justice of Israel's cause. I do not believe that Israelis can be united unless Israel acts morally and justly.

Three clarifications are needed. First, "unity" is not inconsistent with pluralism. Israel cannot expect and need not have a position which everyone accepts. There is no great harm if there are substantial fringes of opinion deeply in disagreement, so long as the center, including a large share of the intellectual community, strongly believes in itself and what the country is doing, and sees the fringes as fringes, not as the "true conscience of the country."

Second, there does not need to be agreement about the details of policy, or even all major elements of policy. The unity is necessary only about Israel's fundamental position, and about the recognition that the other issues are tactical.

Third, and most important, "justice" must be understood in a mature way. A serious conception of "justice" depends on an understanding of the history and character of the Middle East and of the forces influencing the situation within which Israel must act. Full justice is rarely possible, and certainly not soon in the Middle East. When I say that Israel must act justly in order to survive, I do not mean that Israel must do the impossible and produce justice; rather that Israel must do what is just for it to do. This will not be enough to bring full justice to the region and its peoples. Israel must act justly; it cannot be called on to produce justice.

Since the pursuit of peace and of security for Israel depends upon its pursuit of justice, what does justice require of Israel in its dealings with the Palestinians?

The Palestinians are victims. They are oppressed, and do not have the freedom to choose their own government. They deserve our sympathy, and are entitled to the protection we are

113

commanded to provide for the weak and disadvantaged. But this does not mean that they are innocent or admirable, or that we must pretend that they are. To do justice to them we have to understand them realistically as well as sympathetically. Partly this is because we must do justice to ourselves as well, and partly this is because you cannot do lasting good for a person or a people if you pretend he or they are what they are not. We are commanded to help the weak and nasty, not just good people. Part of our obligation to respect the humanity even of our enemies is recognizing their potential to become better people. But respecting people's potential to become better does not mean denying the way that they are now.

One of the things that the *intifada* represents is a human testing of the Israelis by the Palestinians. The Palestinian crowds are saying very forcefully to the Israelis: "we hate you, we want you to go away and leave us alone. You cannot stay here unless you have the will to withstand our hate." The emotional intensity of the Arab crowds came as a shock to the Israeli soldiers. They had not fully realized or remembered the human meaning of occupation, even benign occupation. And most of them paid little attention to those Israelis who have consistently tried to teach their fellow citizens about the depth and intensity of Arab hatred for Israel. The Arabs could see that the soldiers were taken aback; that they were uncomfortable about having to resist this massive human feeling, and many were shocked to find themselves hated. In the local press and the statements of many Israeli politicians and public figures, and in the world press, the Palestinians were reinforced, and at first they seemed to be getting some good results — in return for costs that were in Arab accounting quite low, since they have always been ready to pay with the bodies and lives of their children.

It is unjust — certainly unfortunate — that the Palestinians do not have a state of their own and that the Palestinians living in the territories do not have self-determination. To decide how much this injustice is influencing the states and foreign leaders who have protested against it, we need to check how much they have protested against the greater injustice against the Kurds, who also do not have a state or self-determination. There are many more Kurds than Palestinians, and Kurdish nationalism is much older and stronger than Palestinian nationalism. The Kurds, who are forced to live under Turkish, Iraqi, Syrian, and Iranian rule, although they are the great majority of people living in the single piece of territory which would be Kurdistan if it were not occupied by four other countries, are generally treated much worse than the Palestinians under Israeli rule. Recently, for example, Iraq used poison gas to massacre thousands of Kurds. The lack of concern about Kurdish rights — and those of more than a dozen other peoples with equally strong claims who lack their own state and self-determination — strongly suggests that some of those who are speaking up for the Palestinians are moved by feelings other than just a concern for justice.

But world inconsistency and duplicity do not absolve Israel of responsibility for acting justly. It only eliminates "international opinion" as a judge or even commentator. We Jews have to decide for ourselves what justice requires of us — paying no attention to what "the world says."

There is one way in which a respectable case can be made for seeking to build a Palestinian negotiating partner to seek an agreement about the territories before there is peace with the Arab states (although, even though the case is respectable, I believe it is wrong). This way is first to completely suppress the *intifada* so that the Palestinians of the territories come to a general acceptance of the conclusion that it was a big mistake — that is, that they paid a high price and got nothing in return — and that the Israelis ended up stronger and more united (because an Israeli generation that grew up "innocent" learned of Arab hatred and then, after struggle, came to accept the need to do what it takes to protect their country against that hatred). This depends on Israel visibly deciding that it is quite prepared to do the dirty work of occupation as long as necessary — accepting the task with as much unity and good grace as the other requirements of defense. When all that has happened — when it is clear that throwing stones and molotov cocktails at Israeli troops does not work, that political attacks and foreign accusations of immorality serve only to make Israelis more united and less willing to accept pressure from the U.S. — then it would not be completely crazy for Israel to make some modest efforts (not a desperate commitment) to find a Palestinian negotiating partner.

Most of the people who want Israel to pursue negotiations at this time deny that any of these prerequisites are possible. In fact they base their case primarily on the argument that they are impossible. But we do not have to reject a proposal just because most of its advocates use the wrong arguments. So those who disagree with my conclusions about the best way to pursue peace should continue to advocate negotiating with the Palestinians first, not because we *have to* make peace with them (either for morality or security), but because it is desirable to do so if possible. And to prevent their recommendation from irresponsibly damaging the prospects for peace, they should insist on completely suppressing the *intifada* and demonstrating Israeli willingness and physical and political ability to continue the occupation indefinitely, as necessary prerequisites for their negotiation strategy.

What is the alternative? It is to put down the *intifada* and systematically to call on the Arab states to make peace so that serious negotiations with the Palestinians will become possible. Since it is not likely that this alternative will bring quick results, we need to look at how painful it will be — and whether it is an unjust choice to make.

But before we do that, we should note that it is also true that something else might happen while Israel is carrying out this policy. The Palestinians of the territories might decide that their current leaders and outside "supporters" have failed, and that they have to choose some leaders who will make peace with Israel and negotiate for as favorable conditions as they can get. If this happens, and such a group stands up against the attacks of the PLO and the Islamic fundamentalists, and the Arab states, and the leftwing press and political analysts, Israel should negotiate with it and give it as generous terms as possible. But it would be very harmful to negotiate with ourselves now about just how generous terms we should give. Whether or not such Palestinian leadership arises does not depend on what Israel says about the terms that it will give. It depends on the social strength of the Palestinian community and their willingness to make the very hard decision to accept the reality of their situation, give up dreams and illusions, and, even more difficult, give up the support and domination of those who they have always followed and who have much more power than they do. This is, unfortunately, unlikely to happen.

Part of the reason it is unlikely is that almost everything that the Israeli and other "doves" have been doing works against it. They have not rejected — and usually do not even criticize — Palestinians who refuse to make peace with Israel; they have not told the Palestinians that violent attacks on the occupation will not work; they have rejected as "Uncle Toms" any Palestinians who showed willingness to work with the occupation. Israeli "doves," including much of the leadership of the security forces, thought for a long time, and some of them still do, that the *intifada* would improve the prospects for peace and improve the position of the West Bankers by making Israelis aware of how much the occupation was hated and by making the status quo unacceptable, and putting pressure on Israel to make peace. This shows how poorly they understand and how much harm to their own cause can be done by accepting their proposals.

In fact the *intifada* has been predictably bad for the West Bankers and for the prospects of peace. It has weakened Jordan and the elements of the West Bank community most interested in peace. It has strengthened, at least temporarily, the position of Islamic fundamentalists and others least willing to make peace. It has greatly worsened the quality of life under the occupation, not only during the *intifada* but also by destroying the structure of relationships under which the large degree of practical self-government had developed. Life will be worse for the Palestinians of the territories than it was in November 1987 for a long time, even if Israel goes very far to make it better. Finally, it has given a new lease on life to the Arab states' hope that Israel can be defeated if they continue to hold out against making peace.

Briefly, the argument on justice is that the continuation of the occupation is the fault of the Arab states who refuse to make peace, and that Israel has no choice there than to continue to occupy the territories for some more years. Therefore it is just in the circumstances for Israel to continue to occupy the area (although it is required to do it in a way that realistically minimizes the overall harm to the Palestinians consistent with Israeli security).

If the policy is just and necessary, it should command the loyalty and support of the great mass of Israelis. The young Israeli soldiers who have to do the dirty work should have the moral support of the community, and the teaching and other help they need to learn to act properly.

Sometimes it is said that Israel cannot continue to occupy the territories without "destroying its soul," or in less dramatic terms, without excessive harm to morale or unity. But occupation, even with periodic *intifadas*, is much less costly in both Arab and Jewish lives than wars. Are we really willing to say that occupation duty is so unpleasant that we would accept a greater chance of war to avoid it? Is it really more immoral to use tear gas and expulsions against Palestinians than it is to kill them in a war? It seems clear that if Israel is reasonably united in recognizing the necessity of continued occupation it will see the unpleasantness of occupation as a necessary evil, and there will be no more corrosion of the soul than there is from the necessity of killing young Arabs in combat.

How feasible is this alternative. Can the *intifada* and long-term Palestinian violent resistance to occupation be defeated at an acceptable cost? Is there a serious hope for peace?

We have to recognize that it is likely that there will always be Arab support for violent demonstrations whenever the Israelis whose job it is to suppress such demonstrations show that they feel ambivalent about doing so, and that they are sympathetically moved by the emotional attacks upon them and their country. And it will probably always be easy to organize violent Palestinian demonstrations so long as the demonstrations are seen to be causing serious divisions within Israel. But I believe that Israeli ambivalence and reluctance to accept the necessity of suppressing the *intifada* has largely gone, and that after the election there will be clear support in Israel for defeating the *intifada*.

If no concessions are made as a result of the *intifada*, if the economic costs to the Palestinians are high, and if the leaders and the families of youth leaders, those who organize and agitate, suffer penalties such as jail, house destruction, and/or expulsion, and other sensible measures are taken, then once the *intifada* comes to an end there will be a reasonable degree of peace for a while — violent attacks on Israelis will again be rare.

Even so, if Israel must continue to occupy the territories, it must expect some kind of "uprising" every 5 or 10 or 15 years (if it takes so long to achieve peace). Although if Israel acts promptly, decisively, and with reasonable unity to put down such "uprisings," they are likely to be very much shorter than the *intifada*. The prospect of periodic uprisings is similar to Israel's experience with wars. The lesson of history is that until the Arab states make peace with Israel, Israel cannot stay in the Middle East without expecting to have a war every 10 or 20 years. And many more Israelis and many more Arabs are killed in the wars than in the uprisings. So if Israel can live with wars, it should be able to live with uprisings.

How sullen will the peace between uprisings be? Will Israel have to keep large forces in the territories and will civilians be unable to peaceably visit or pass through the territories? If Israel acts with a modest degree of competence and determination — comparable to that it has shown in the past — Israel will not have to continue to devote large forces to keeping order in the territories.

(And if Israel can devote any political cleverness to the task the chances are much better.) While it is unlikely that the peaceable spirit that we felt when we walked in the territories a dozen years ago will ever return, it is quite possible that enough of a daily practical live-and-let-live attitude will again develop so that Israelis can normally drive or walk in most of the territories without much fear.

What does Israel need to do? For one thing it has to have an explicit peace policy. Peace should be an official and formally stated primary goal of the Israeli government and of the major parties. Israel should say clearly that it does not accept the idea of permanent conflict with its neighbors. This does not mean that the Israeli government has to be impatient or that it always has to claim that it has a way of moving directly to peace. But Israel should have an official and generally accepted view of why it has not achieved peace so far, what the obstacles are, and of the general approach it is using to do what is possible to encourage peace. Such a policy would almost certainly include a regularly restated call on the Arab countries to negotiate peace, and an expression of Israeli readiness to do so. This has to be done with dignity, consistent with Arab expectations of how strong nations should behave if they respect themselves, because if it is done in fawning or excessively eager terms it will be counter-productive.

The reason a peace policy does not mean that Israel should always have a theory of how to achieve peace in the current circumstances is that sometimes peace may be temporarily impossible. A policy that cannot tell when peace is impossible cannot recognize the special circumstances when peace may suddenly become more possible. Obviously, therefore, a peace policy does not mean that Israel must always be trying to arrange negotiations or putting forward new proposals. Patience is just as important as determination and initiative. But at all times Israel must have an analysis of how it is pursuing peace and why, even if the current expression of that policy is to wait. Possibly the more explicit expression of Israel's peace policy would help to bring about the national unity required to defeat the *intifada* and to accept the need to carry the burdens of occupation as long as necessary.

THE POLITICS OF MORALITY AND THE MORALITY OF POLITICS

Bernard Susser

There is a natural human compulsion to seek simplicity and uniformity in concepts and ideas. Ragged edges create cognitive friction and we prefer to avoid them. When cherished and long-held perspectives prove inadequate to some new situation, there is a tendency to bridle at the intellectual disorder that is created. At times, when a consecrated set of rules that has become part of our instinctual repertoire fails us in application or extension, we opt for the most draconic solution of all. Preferring not to clutter our world with complex distinctions and multiple criteria, we simply write off the threatening element; we claim that it frustrates our standards because it is lacking in standards entirely. The recalcitrant area that violated our expectations is, in a sense, punished for its waywardness. If it does not fit the rules, it is deemed unfit for rule-governed discourse.

Much of the history of Machiavellian *raison d'etat* is, I believe, of this kind. The rise of nationalism and of the modern nation-state forced the unsettling recognition that standards of personal morality — so severe and demanding in the Christian Middle Ages — were often inapplicable to the demands of public life. Power over the destiny of great collectivities, it became clear, could not effectively be wielded within the constraints imposed by the "golden rule," to say nothing of the call to "turn the other cheek." Coercion — not love or solidarity or justice — was the hard currency of public life.

The elementary requisites of diplomacy patently conflicted with the obligation to speak the whole truth and avoid all forms of deviousness. Sovereignty demanded dealing pitilessly with the mutinous, large scale organization precluded care for that inevitable minority who suffered from even the most just of laws, the distribution of public resources was ineluctably at the expense of some and to the benefit of others and, perhaps above all, the threat and the practice of war involved activities that were egregious by the criteria of personal morality.

Three broad choices were available to those who confronted

this vexing quandary. First, public life could be compelled, nevertheless, to suit itself to the familiar demands of personal morality despite the conspicuous asymmetry between them. This choice was doomed either to deteriorate into hypocrisy or to end in a horrified shrinking from the corrupting imperatives of politics. Notably, very few have been willing to defend this first choice at a sophisticated level of ethical discourse (although it must be said parenthetically that there has never been a dearth of those who were only too happy to applaud it warmly and then disregard it in practice).

Far more common was the second alternative: if the moral rules that bound us as individuals were basically inapplicable to the demands of statecraft, then so be it. The state was declared to be beyond the orbit of morality; it revolved on its own axis and hence was beholden to no rules but those that were of its own making. Beyond the borders of personal morality lay the wasteland. This is the "draconic" solution of which I spoke at the outset. An habitual standard fails us and rather than entertain the demanding idea of a complex, highly differentiated solution, we stick to our familiar guns. The fault, so this second position claims, lies not in the inadequacy or partiality of our moral outlook as individuals but rather in the unyielding depravity of public life.

There is, notably, a significant nexus between these two choices and the Christian tradition that begot them. With its disparaging views on worldly power, its characterization of the world of politics as the domain of "untruth," its identification of the state and its instrumentalities with the "fall," it should occasion little surprise that statecraft, in Christian thought, was so often dissociated from moral earnestness. Paradoxically, although Machiavelli was excoriated by the Christian establishment, his amoral appreciation of the public domain derives in no small measure from a transfiguration of common Christian perceptions.

That Christianity set unattainable, well-nigh otherworldly standards in personal morality — loving one's enemies, turning the other cheek, the derogation of the carnal, etc. — only widened the abyss between the ethics of individual life and of the public domain. For if moral counsels such as "do unto others as you would have others do unto you" and "justice, justice shall you pursue" are not flagrantly inappropriate to political conduct, loving one's enemies and turning the other cheek surely are. Their import and purpose is, in fact, to extol the anti-political, i.e., to dramatize the inevitable opposition between public life's mundane constraints and the spiritual perfection of the Christian soul. That politics was abandoned to cynical counsels such as "might makes right" was, therefore, not an unforeseeable eventuality.

There is, however, a third choice, a typically complex and demanding choice that will not suit those who like their morality catechismically short and conveniently simple. It admits outright that the standards appropriate to public life often cannot be reproduced mechanically from the conventions that control our individual conduct. While private and public ethics often overlap and reinforce each other, they do, at times, necessarily part company. But it denies that, having made this admission, politics is condemned to become a law unto itself, or, more accurately, a lawlessness unto itself.

Statecraft is subject to an ethics that is uniquely its own, to standards that are none the less moral for being inappropriate to private life. Like individuals, states can act nobly or basely, virtuously or viciously. (This is said not as a vacuous preachment, but rather as a description of the world that we all recognize.) In a word, politics is never merely politics; it is always human action with all the human standards appertaining thereunto. Any ethical teaching large enough to accommodate the richness of human experience must account for and flesh out the parallel but not always overlapping standards that belong respectively to the private and the public spheres.

Nor is there any justification in inferring from the above that public ethics, because of its departures from individual morality, is somehow a lesser or laxer code. In truth, the ethical demands of public life are, in certain respects, incomparably more exacting than those we accept in personal conduct. If we forgive ourselves and our associates the occasional peccadillo without the moral roof falling down around our heads, we react quite differently to the public official who takes a bribe only "on occasion." If in private life we do everything in our power to minimize risks to our physical well-being, as citizens we are called to serve our country in the most dangerous of circumstances — even to sacrifice our lives for the well-being of others. In private life our narrow interests as individuals and families are our chief concern; as tax-paying citizens we part with our possessions for the good of the whole.

A systematically exhaustive account of morality in the public sphere would involve a lifetime's industry for the greatest of minds. The task is so overwhelming that I shrink from even considering its simplest elements. Yet, if the construction of a theoretical framework appropriate to this undertaking is an intimidating prospect — worthy of the likes of a Hugo Grotius or, perhaps, a John Rawls in our time — this is no reason to throw up one's hands in despair. Although quite formidable and not a little daunting, it appears feasible, at least at the practical level, to formulate a few guidelines that seem basic to the morality of collectivities such as states and nations in their relations with one another.

Three broad and interlocking (but alas, hardly precise) principles seem unavoidable.

First: Nationalism, as the expression of a collectivity's unique "being," is indispensable to its survival, identity and healthy self-assertion. Indeed, in the service of collective well-being, the state's conduct is not invariably subject to the prohibitions that limit individual action. And yet, an aggressive and narcissistic nationalism that swallows all other standards to become the single focus and exclusive criterion for action, suffers from the dangerous moral infirmity of collective egoism. To forget that the national community is a part of the international community of nations, to lose sight of one's responsibilities to the broader collective of humankind, is the prelude to moral disaster.

Second: The rights, needs, desires and interests of other groups have a presumptive claim to be respected in our actions. The more critical these rights, needs, etc., are to their welfare or survival, the more they properly impinge on our moral responsibilities. This is not to say, of course, that all such needs must be honored in practice or that they are equal in standing to those that significantly affect our own welfare. It does, however, entail the far from trivial responsibility to weigh and measure (with no less earnestness than one would expect from others) the ramifications of a decision on all those it may affect.

Factoring the needs of others into a political decision guarantees no particular results; no algorythmic table for such calculations can be specified in advance of a concrete problem situation. What can be specified in advance is only the principle: the needs of others have significant standing in the relations between collectivities. Barring compelling reasons of state and of national interest, they cannot be overlooked. And even when they must be overridden, this decision is properly arrived at at the end of a serious moral exercise rather than casually assumed at its outset. A state's moral "quotient," as it were, consists in the seriousness with which it considers and includes the needs of others in its own political calculations.

There are, of course, many cases where, felicitously, pragmatic and moral considerations coincide. In these fortunate coincidences, a collectivity's ethical character is not put to the test. Where honesty (or compassion or fair-dealing) is good policy, the moral moment is hardly called into play. By contrast, when they find themselves on opposing sides of our political deliberations, the full range of our human loyalties are pressed into service. To repeat: moral considerations need not, in the end, override our pragmatic concerns or determine our decisions. They do, nevertheless, possess autonomous and irreducible standing in the tribunal of human political judgement.

Third: The relationship between means and ends should be approached neither exclusively as a question of tactics (means) nor yet as if it were purely a question of moral desirables (ends). As the two complementary foci of this classic dilemma indicate, it is inevitably a compound question, one that achieves its full stature only when appreciated in relational terms: the relation of means to ends. Both the non-political preacher of moralisms and the amoral practitioner of power politics miss the uniquely demanding nature of political morality. Only when means and ends are comprehended as an integral composite is the fully human context of statecraft actually revealed. Here, the constraints of principle and the constraints of practice must jointly accept responsibility for decisions taken.

It is surely true that unacceptable means (e.g., by the standards of principles one and/or two) tend to corrupt even the most morally unimpeachable end. There is sober wisdom in the adage that the quality of the means utilized conditions the quality of the ends achieved. And yet, subjecting the tactical question exclusively to the lofty standards of the ends aspired to will, in most cases, be tantamount to forfeiting, in advance, the attainment of these desired ends.

Politics, as human action, offers more than these stunted alternatives. It acknowledges and accepts both the permanent tension and the inevitable coexistence that marks the relationship between moral sensitivity and political shrewdness. It addresses the political actor both as a partisan and as a moral agent — nothing less is adequate to the manifold character of human action. Although this decision process defies systematization, precision or pre-knowledge, it engages the gamut of sensibilities, from the most parochial of our interests to the most universal of our ethical commitments.

But what of the challenge of moral relativism? How, the editor queries, can we speak of "ultimate ethical commitments" if these commitments are recognized as artifacts peculiar to unique ethical environments, historical periods and human contexts, when we understand them as social constructions rather than objective givens? This, I believe, is the least of our worries. Although relativism, in all its many forms, may well be the central problem of all contemporary philosophy, it remains just that, a "philosophical" problem. As such, it saddles the modern theoretical intelligence with what is, doubtless, the knottiest and most intractable of difficulties. As a pragmatic matter, however, it is of only marginal concern. It belongs to the stuff of parody to picture political figures facing a crucial ethical issue writhing with intellectual indecision, paralyzed with contemplation because they recognize that other cultures follow different moral standards. As a practical political question, relativism is, for the very most part, an intellectual scarecrow.

No more than the ultimately arbitrary sounds of the English language prevent its being spoken fluently by even linguists who study just this question: Does the ultimately relative nature of human moral constructions prevent even a self-conscious philosopher from being an adept of a particular moral environment? The "what if I had been born a ......?" questions belong to sophomoric soul-searching, not to the political struggles of great collectivities. Faced with a decision, we inexorably draw on the resources that are ours — not because we have endowed these resources with privileged theoretical standing but simply because we have no other resources on which to draw. Indecision, when it does paralyze, derived from a conflict of values or objectives *within* a tradition, not from the abstractions of the sociology of knowledge.

All of the above has been in the nature of a rambling and heuristic exploration rather than a programmatic exposition. It has also been pitched to the broadest of concerns, or, in other words, I have deliberately avoided addressing the painful issues that form the unspoken context to this series of essays. Still, one crucial corollary to the three principles explored above requires enunciation if this discussion is not to remain an aesthetic-philosophic fiddling while the streets burn and the stones fly.

Moral responsibility, or at least the bulk of it, rests on the fundamental orientation a collectivity chooses to follow in pursuing its objectives. These broad orientations and the first principles on which they rest engage the wheels of practice in a variety of ways. Invariably, the imperatives of practice raise their own subsidiary moral dilemmas. These, however, cannot be judged as self-standing issues or scrutinized apart from the principles of which they are a consequence.

To illustrate: a political community chooses to pursue its goals oblivious of the rights of others (in the context of principle two above). Not surprisingly, it soon finds itself confronted by hostile resistance that raises a host of moral dilemmas. There is, at this point, little sense and much sham moralizing in crying holy and meek at the distressing ethical binds that must now be faced. To narrow moral concern to the actions of those who need to deal with the outcomes of principled decisions is to do violence to moral judgement. It is also to (perhaps cynically) distract attention from the decision to its consequences. The initiator of this volume is to be praised for returning the moral question to the level of principle where it properly belongs.

IS THE MORALITY OF POLITICAL COMMUNITIES THE SAME AS THE MORALITY OF INDIVIDUALS? — YES AND NO

Mervin F. Verbit

Most commentators on Israel's handling of the territories which came under her rule as a result of the Six-Day War fall into two categories, especially since the beginning of the *intifada*. There are the vindicators, who can see no Israeli wrong or who minimize and excuse it when it confronts them starkly, and the soul-searchers, who treat every choice among evils as a pact with Satan and transform every personal transgression into national immorality. Both of these perspectives draw on the Jewish experience for validation, but both do so as if 4,000 years yielded only one lesson, and a simple one at that. If good and evil were as impervious to each other in behavior as they are distinct in conceptualization, then monochromatic evaluations might have some merit. As things are, however, both the vindicators and the soul-searchers invite dismissal from people who seriously attempt to subject politics to morality with due recognition of the complexity of both. The present symposium, therefore, is a welcome opportunity to consider Israel's recent stance in a systematic way without foregone conclusions.

Is the morality applicable to political communities (and, most particularly, to states) the same as the morality of individuals? That question is best answered by the conventional Jewish "Yes and No." On the one hand, to propose two disparate sets of moral standards would be suspect in that it would sound like an attempt to justify behavior which is morally insupportable. In the end, after all, it is individuals who act, and we, perhaps better than most people, know how much evil can be done when ugly deeds are cloaked in pretty theories about society as a whole.

On the other hand, a society is more than the sum of the individuals in it. Its characteristics are more than their traits averaged, and its requirements are more than their desires summed. The realization that a collectivity has its own life is the very foundation of social science, as well as a central element in virtually all legal traditions, which treat corporations and political jurisdictions as entities. Indeed, most people understand the difference between the needs of a society and those of its members. It is that understanding which, for example, induces middlebrows to support high culture and make laymen want their clergy to be more pious. Also, the state can compel behaviors that no individual may impose on another and can provide benefits which no private philanthropy can approach. The state, moreover, has a monopoly on the legitimate use of force for control and punishment.

Since the individual and the state are inherently different in their respective needs, responsibilities, and powers, they cannot properly be subjected to the same morality. However, if individual and collective moralities are utterly distinct, then the very notion of morality loses all content. There is one morality, but it must be applied *mutatis mutandis.*

The proper framework for consideration of Israel's administration of the territories is self-defense, which was the context in which the territories were acquired and which remains Israel's dominant concern. The guiding vision of the Arabs has from the beginning been Israel's dissolution. What the Arabs have differed over is how that goal was to be achieved — politically or militarily, in stages or in one major effort. The *intifada* is defined by its leaders as part of the war against Israel, and that is what it is, even though its immediate goal seems to have been to win public opinion rather than military victory. We hope, of course, that the activities of the PLO in November and December 1988 mean that those Arabs who have despaired of destroying Israel and are, consequently, prepared to postpone realization of their dreams to a "messianic" future and in the meantime accept what they see as a less than ideal arrangement have become powerful enough to control Palestinian affairs. However, until that hopeful interpretation is tested in behavior over time with convincing positive results, self-defense must remain the most salient concern of Israeli policy.

Individuals have the right to protect themselves from assault, a right which is rooted in the ultimate value of human life and in the equal dignity of all human beings. States, too, have the right of self-preservation. Moreover, self-realization, or self-determination, is increasingly coming to be recognized as a right of all groups with a significant collective identity. The problem is that full Jewish national self-realization and full Palestinian national self-realization are incompatible. The crucial difference is that the Jews have always sought peaceful compromise even when it would entail giving up part of their historical claim, and the Palestinians never considered peaceful compromise. The individual exceptions on both sides have been just that — exceptions; they have never been even close to effective control of their respective societies. Whether we are now witnessing a change in this pattern among Palestinians remains for the future to determine. Our present analysis concerns the past and the present, in which the Palestinians' plan for achieving their self-realization has threatened the very existence of the Jewish state.

How may an individual defend himself morally against life-threatening assault, and how does our answer to that question apply to states? The ideal, of course, is to persuade an assailant voluntarily to end the threat because of self-interest or, less likely, moral principle. Failing that, four graduated levels of response can be identified: 1) enough force to escape; 2) enough force to persuade the assailant that his threatening behavior exposes him to unacceptable risk; 3) enough force to incapacitate the assailant, that is, to make him unable to pose a threat; and 4) enough force to kill the assailant. Certainly, the moral approach is to use the lowest level of force likely to provide effective self-defense, and that principle holds for states as for individuals.

The options available to states and to individuals are, however, not identical. Escape is sometimes possible in confrontations between individuals but is obviously irrelevant when a threat is directed against a state. That leaves the three remaining levels of response in ascending order of harshness and descending order of moral desirability. The moral way for Israel to behave, then, is first to try to persuade her enemies that it will serve them well economically, politically, and culturally to live in peace with Israel. Israel has done, and continues to do, this. However, since that effort has not succeeded, Israel would be expected to make clear to her enemies that any attempt at Israel's destruction will result in greater losses for them than they are willing to endure. For many who wish Israel's dissolution, that level of response is sufficient deterrent. For others it is not, and therefore we would expect Israel to move to the next level and act so as to incapacitate those who persist in actively threatening her.

By and large, this graduated approach, using all three levels simultaneously and directing each one to that segment of the Arab population likely to be affected by it, has characterized Israel's response. It has shaped Israel's policy and has guided Israel's instructions to her soldiers. Indeed, occasionally (some would say as a general pattern) Israel may respond to danger too mildly to be effective, thus prolonging the threat and leading to heightened embarrassment and eventually to the need for still harsher measures. Also, it should be recognized that the levels of response can entail different actions when collective than when individual. Sometimes, threatened states or movements cannot be convinced about the risks to themselves or cannot be incapacitated except in ways that entail the death of some of their members. In such cases, the application of what is middle-range force at the collective level includes what is the most extreme (lethal) force at the individual level. When that happens, what is forbidden to individuals may, nevertheless, be the preferable option for a state and, consequently, for the state's agents.

Inevitably, governmental policy is not implemented in every case with unexceptional judgment or adhered to with total consistency. It is clear that occupation breeds fear where one would like security, contempt where one would like respect, resentment — even hatred where one would like friendship. The problem is exacerbated when the occupied population wants the occupier not just out, but politically and perhaps literally dead, and the occupier knows that any significant gathering of strength by the occupied may indeed bring about that end. What is more, in any society some people will be driven by such motives as economic exploitation, jingoistic imperialism, or the sheer psychological satisfaction of domination over others, and will use whatever situation presents itself to play out these motives. Israel's public culture, educational system, and military socialization all condemn these motives and convey that only self-defense requires, justifies, and shapes the nature of rule over the Arab population in the territories. When Israelis do commit error, or worse, Israel almost always takes action to reaffirm, publicly and/or institutionally, its moral position. Whether she does so with appropriately severe penalties is a matter of controversy. That she does so at all, especially under the circumstances, is remarkable.

To the question of whether moral positions are absolutist or relativistic, the answer is also conventionally Jewish: "Both!" Values are absolute. If cultures vary in their values, as they do, that does not make all values equally valid. It makes some cultures more moral than others. Even where successful headhunting yields honor and status, life is sacred; the head-hunters just do not know it. Even in a culture which excessively rewards devotion to one's own advancement at almost any cost, integrity and concern for others are right. In morality, it has been remarked, God plus one make a majority.

Values are also relative. The claim that values are relative to the situation is really a shorthand way of recognizing that values are in fact relative to other values. The "situation" is that two (or more) values often cannot be implemented simultaneously. When the truth hurts, is it better to cause pain or to lie for compassion's sake? When justice and mercy collide, which takes precedence? When may a person kill in order to save his own life? The only way to make values operative is to understand that they often, perhaps usually, compete with one another in the morally challenging situations that constitute most of life. The moral decision among *absolute* values is, thus, *relative* to the varying situations in which those values make their respective claims. In the case under review here, morality weights actions against the danger to which those actions are offered as a defense.

In this less than perfect world, our choices are often between bad and worse. When that is the case, it is good to choose the bad over the worse. We are morally secure as long as we remember that, when we so choose, we are commanded to repent for deeds which, considering the alternatives, are virtuous. The paradox is that we must often lament behavior which is commendable as we commend behavior which is lamentable. I believe that that paradox is understood by most Israelis most of the time and by Israel as a society all of the time.

MORALITY AND ISRAELI POLICY IN THE TERRITORIES

Harold M. Waller

It is hardly surprising that the question of the morality of Israel's policies in Judea, Samaria, and Gaza should have been raised during the course of the uprising of the Palestinians that began in December 1987. The actions taken by the authorities to cope with the uprising were often harsh and surely unpleasant. In some cases individual soldiers or groups of them engaged in conduct that was wrong. On several occasions punishments were meted out. The major problem, however, was the wide dissemination of pictures and television film of Israeli troops in action, trying to quell demonstrations, stone-throwing, and fire-bombing by what appeared to be mainly groups of teenagers. Many people, both inside and outside of Israel, friends of Israel and those not so friendly, became upset at purported violations of human rights and behavior that they considered to have gone beyond the bounds of the moral.

The criticisms necessitate considered examination of the issues involved, especially the assumptions employed by those on various sides of the issue. Although no single contribution to this symposium is likely to answer all of the relevant questions, the total effort should bring some light to a vexing subject.

Certain points must be made clear at the outset. First of all, implicit in many attacks on Israeli behavior is the assumption that any action by the authorities against the inhabitants is inherently immoral because Israel has no business being in the territories in the first place. The argument may be preposterous, but it is nevertheless one with which we must contend. If one accepts the proposition that Israel was responding appropriately to provocations that amounted to a *casus belli* by Egypt and defending itself against unprovoked aggression by Jordan and Syria in 1967, then the occupation of territories that fell under Israeli control is undoubtedly legal and I think moral as well. The war that Israel fought was not an aggressive invasion nor a war of conquest. It was a war of self-defense. The fact that in the course of such a war Israel found itself in control of new territories is a common outcome of a war and is certainly not immoral, unless one takes the position that war per se, with no distinction between aggressive and defensive war, is immoral. Israel's occupation of the territories is no less moral than the occupation of Germany and Japan by the victorious Allies after World War II.

The key question is what happened after the war. In this connection there are two considerations: Israel's long-term behavior as legal occupying power and Israel's short-term behavior in dealing with the uprising. Each of these issues will be considered in turn. Meanwhile it is necessary to bear in mind a distinction between a good or wise policy and a moral policy. A policy that does not violate standards of morality may not necessarily constitute an intelligent policy. In view of the fact that our task here is to evaluate the morality of Israeli policy, the question of the wisdom of particular policies will not be addressed. Thus we are not concerned that Israel's policies were right or smart or intelligent, only whether they were moral.

From the foregoing, if a war is just and is prosecuted in order to resist or forestall aggression, a consequent occupation of territory that does not belong to the victorious state should be considered moral. Moreover, the victorious state does not have an obligation to return any or all of the territory to the previous owner. (In the case of Judea, Samaria, and Gaza, there was no previous owner in any meaningful legal sense.) However, I do believe that there is an obligation to terminate a state of war and any attendant occupation through the conclusion of a peace treaty. A treaty may involve the permanent transfer of some territory from one ownership to another. If that is so, such a transfer would not be immoral. The problem is that if there is a victor and a vanquished, can a treaty be concluded that is not imposed? An imposed peace may well involve elements of immorality.

The question of an imposed peace is not a new one. In the absence of a binding international dispute-settling mechanism it is difficult to guarantee that the content of an imposed peace would be moral. (There are those who would argue that even international intervention would not insure a moral peace.) Ultimately that question requires an individual judgment, although we could attempt to articulate some of the principles that might guide such judgments. At this juncture it should be sufficient to note that the question of morality in international politics has never been resolved effectively. As outside observers we can try to make distinctions between just and unjust wars, between moral and immoral behavior during the course of a war, between permissible behavior and war crimes. We can even argue that nations should be guided in their actions by considerations of morality as well as national interest. But if a political leader were confronted with what he or she perceived as a conflict between morality and what the national interest required, what would the likely outcome be?

An important issue that arises from this discussion is what happens when an occupation, which by definition is temporary, is converted into a permanent acquisition by the victorious state. Assuming that the original occupation was legal and moral, can the winner unilaterally declare the territory in question to be part of his state? That would certainly violate international norms or morality, although it must be noted that the international community does not lack hypocrites. Many of those countries who most vociferously advocate the principle of the inadmissibility of the acquisition of territory by force, as articulated in UN Resolution 242, for example, do themselves include territory that was acquired by force. Nevertheless that is the principle to which the international community at least pays lip service today. Therefore one must conclude that it is immoral to convert an occupation unilaterally into a permanent part of the victorious state, although the ceding of territory in the context of a peace treaty may be acceptable.

In this light, what can one say about Israel's actions that applied Israeli law to the eastern part of Jerusalem in 1967 and to the Golan Heights in 1980? With respect to Jerusalem, the territory was never part of a sovereign state and it was used as a launching pad for aggression against Israel. Therefore there should be no question of morality regarding its incorporation into the state. Whether it was a good policy decision is a separate matter, and not our concern in this symposium. The Golan Heights are another matter. It is one thing for Israel to assert that it intends to demand, in the course of peace negotiations with Syria, that the Heights be ceded because Israel is unwilling to risk the security threat of having Syrian troops up there again. (Of course it could be argued that that objective could be achieved without annexation.) It is quite another thing to incorporate the territory unilaterally. That certainly does raise questions of morality, although Syria surely was an aggressor in 1967 and aggression should not be without cost. On the other hand, pronouncements about the Golan by Israeli political leaders notwithstanding, Israel presumably remains willing to negotiate a peace treaty with Syria on the basis of

Resolution 242 with all that implies. Thus it would be fair to say that it is premature to declare Israel's actions with regard to the Golan as immoral unless and until Syria indicated a willingness to negotiate peace directly with Israel and Israel refused to negotiate. As yet that has not occurred.

Another general consideration is the question of whether morality can be suspended for *raison d'etat*. Are there situations where a government leader may feel compelled to do something which he or she considers to be morally wrong because the national interest requires it? This is not simply a question of international relations, because the question can arise domestically as well. For example, it is widely believed that a crisis situation may arise where a decision-maker overrides a constitutional protection, perhaps a fundamental freedom, in order to achieve an objective that is considered to be of a higher order. In this context it should be noted that Canada's constitution includes an override provision (the notwithstanding clause) that enables the federal Parliament and provincial legislatures to enact laws that ordinarily would be unconstitutional violations of individual liberty by invoking the clause. This clause has been invoked on several occasions and was even used routinely by the Quebec National Assembly for a period of years.

What is crucial in considering the question of "suspending morality" is the establishment of a hierarchy of values. If a consensus can be found, it would be recognized that there can be conflicting moral positions unless such a hierarchy is clear. Whether an individual state can establish such a hierarchy of values that would be recognized universally is another matter. For example, is the survival of a particular nation-state a moral value for all people? What about a proposed secession? Is maintaining the integrity of the existing state a high moral value? It may be for the majority of the people in the state, but perhaps not for the minority and for many outsiders. The point is that it is exceedingly difficult to articulate absolute moral principles in international politics. The attempt to do so is not a novelty, but the record of success in this regard is not impressive, even in such an enlightened age as ours.

It should be evident that there is a distinction between individual morality and the collective morality of the state. There may well be moral principles that should guide states, but we understand them less well than we do the principles that guide individuals. It is not that our traditional sources of moral behavior lack references to the morality of collectivities. Rather it is the complexity of collective action compared to individual action, coupled with our inability to enforce a moral order on states that has created this problem. We have developed our sense of individual morality to a greater extent because of our attempt to enshrine moral principles in laws that are enforceable. Thus lawmakers and judges have had to contend with these issues for centuries. I am not suggesting that any nation's body of laws be equated with morality, but obviously there is considerable overlap. Legislators do not pass laws regulating human behavior by dreaming them up inside their heads. Their ideas on such matters are derived from their understanding of moral principles. Regrettably we have not had the same experience in international relations. In fact, the traditional view is that moral principles should not be decisive in that arena. Consequently, I would argue that while individuals, even those acting on behalf of the state, should adhere to moral standards in their behavior, at present it is naive, and perhaps unreasonable to expect states to do the same. We do want state decision-makers to select informed moral choices, but we would find it difficult to specify the principles from which the choices should be derived. Therefore the recourse to moral arguments by individuals, or even states, when evaluating a state's behavior is often no more than a thinly disguised political argument. Furthermore, one must be wary about trying to apply a Nuremberg analogy. The aftermath of the war against the Nazis may well have been a unique historical situation, one in which a large number of states were able to agree (after the fact, it should be noted) as to what constituted immoral and illegal behavior.

What about decision-makers under duress or facing a crisis? Assuming that we want them to act morally and that we can specify the relevant moral principles, the best response is that we must try to specify them in advance and try to establish a hierarchy of values. We cannot depend on the individual's moral formation to prepare him or her for crisis decision-making. Of course that means that someone has to anticipate situations that may arise and others have to try to work out the moral dilemmas. That kind of activity is something that governments ought to be doing, though I doubt that many would be prepared to propose a budget line for moral development. The stress here is on anticipatory morality rather than the imposition of moral standards after an action has taken place. In general the latter practice is dubious, although it might be exemplary, as in the case of the Nazis. But either way, how does one enforce morality in public life? We can provide means of punishing government officials for violations of the law, but what about what used to be called moral turpitude? Perhaps a procedure analogous to the American impeachment process would be appropriate. Such a process would be applied within a state. Is there a way of dealing with immorality on an international basis? Experience to date has not been encouraging. The expectation is that any international process would become politicized. Therefore, the assurance of morality for now probably requires self-policing within states.

Underlying this discussion is the assumption that it is probably meaningless to try to deal with an absolute morality in this context. The smaller the community, the easier it is to establish moral principles that will be widely shared. In the world community this is impossible at present (perhaps the Messianic Era will be different). Inevitably then we are stuck with moral relativism, aside perhaps from a small number of principles. As a result, I am not optimistic about our ability to establish a wide-ranging moral order. In addition I wonder whether a political leader, or anyone living in the real world of politics, can adhere to a morally absolutist position. Assuming for the moment that a religious person should be more moral than an ordinary mortal our experience with religious people in politics, be they popes, ayatollahs, or chief rabbis, has not been ennobling.

After all this, what can be said about the morality of Israel's behavior in the territories since 1967 and especially during 1987-1988? Despite all the criticisms of Israel to which we have been exposed, I find nothing inherently immoral in the occupation itself. This is not a case of the subjection of a people against their will, even if the residents of the territories would like to be rid of Israel. Nor is it a case of oppression or suppression of rights. Occupations are by their nature not very pleasant periods. But Israel's is justified on the basis of its origins. So long as Israel stands ready to conclude peace treaties that would terminate the state of occupation and is prepared to negotiate without preconditions, the question of morality is not applicable. As for the policy toward the uprising, occupied territory is not the same as a colony. There is no moral principle that makes the right of occupied people to revolt a higher value than the obligation of the occupier to maintain public order. In fact, international morality such as it is, expressly imposes such an obligation on the occupying power. Certainly resistance and partisan groups had a right to revolt against German occupation during World War II. And the German response frequently exceeded the bounds of morality. But anyone who suggests a parallel to the situation of Israel in the territories is intellectually dishonest. Germany waged aggressive war and had no business occupying those countries. Israel came into control of the territories in the course of defending itself. That is a fundamental difference. Consequently Israel is justified by any moral standard in taking the necessary steps to maintain public order so long as the methods employed are not inherently immoral.

Israel has also been criticized because some of its soldiers have violated accepted moral standards in individual and group acts. So long as these acts are not state policy and are punished when detected, Israel can be comfortable with its moral position.

The question of morality in public policy is intimidating. One must often grapple with issues of great complexity and gravity. Israel's control over the territories has surely created difficult problems. But these problems are largely matters of policy, not morality.

THE DILEMMAS OF MORALITY AND POWER: A LAST WORD

Daniel J. Elazar

Ours is a topic that can only be talked about today in light of the hard realities of the world in which we live and of the position of the Jews and the Jewish state in that world. Today, we Jews are confronted with the realities of power, its joys and curses.

In some respects we Jews have been reveling in the joys of power, of having power, after such a long period of powerlessness. But now we also have to come to understand some of the curses of power so that we can perhaps understand better what the responsibilities for exercising power are and how difficult these matters can be. It is a lot easier for Jewish intellectuals in America to complain about Irish cops than it is when the Jews are the cops as well. But you cannot have power without having cops. Pio Baroja, the great Spanish anarchist writer of the beginning of the twentieth century, defined the ideal commonwealth from an anarchist point of view as one "without priests, without flies, and without policemen." Unfortunately, we have since learned that one cannot have a world without flies and also have a world without policemen. Somebody has got to make sure that those people who are basically garbage dumpers do not do it. That is at the most minimum level of order, which is why Pio Baroja is now remembered more as a writer than he is as a political thinker.

Jews were in a situation where, figuratively and often literally, we had no policemen for almost 2,000 years. It is not that we were not involved in politics; we were involved in the politics of powerlessness. It was the politics of maneuver, of doing what we could with what little we had, what little we could offer in exchange for a minimum amount of security that enabled us to survive as a people throughout the long years of dispersion.

In many respects, rabbinic Judaism as we came to know it in its normative state was a set of prescriptions for how to live in a world in which we were nearly powerless. The sages did not want a powerless Jewish people, but understood that under the circumstances they needed to teach their people how to reconcile the realities of being in a position of minimal power with their collective needs and how to adjust accordingly. What they did was to teach Jews how to channel their political yearnings into spiritual ones wherever possible. Jews accepted that because they had no choice. While there was a choice, normative Judaism was not as normative as it later became. It struggled with other understandings of how to be Jewish and what being Jewish meant. But at a certain point because there was no other choice it became the normative brand of Judaism, with various variations, but basically that was it.

Approximately 100 years ago, a significant body of Jews founded the Zionist movement on the premise that Jews had had enough of powerlessness; that the Jewish people had to make it their business to get back into a situation where, as a polity, they could exercise normal political power in the normal world. In other words, they argued that the Jewish people should seek a state of its own, one which, whatever special qualities it would have (and there were a wide range of Zionist visions), would be normal, with both the trappings and the responsibilities of sovereignty, with an army, with a police force.

After the Six-Day War, Israel passed from having attained a politics of power to a situation which Jews began, the truth be told, to get a little drunk on power, both in Israel and in the diaspora. Suddenly Jews began discussing Jewish politics in new terms. While acknowledging that the exercise of power is a heavy responsibility, basically Jews liked the new situation very much. We liked being the strong guys on the block for a change. That is most understandable. When all is said and done, it is still better to be the strong guy on the block than the weak guy, even though strength carries with it responsibilities that bring their own problems. That is where we were for the past twenty years.

Now in the last few years Jews have begun to confront the other side of power. It is most blatant, of course, in relation to Israel, but it is not only in relation to Israel. We can see other facets of it, even in relation to diaspora communities, particularly in the United States and France. We are learning that power is like fire. Power is amoral. It is energy, it is force. It can be used for good; it can be used for ill. It can be well-controlled; it can be poorly controlled. It can be well-directed; it can be channeled; if not properly controlled or channeled, it can be abused.

In my opinion, the Jewish people made the right decision 100 years ago when we decided to go back to seek a politics of power, to seek the restoration of our own state that would play a role in the world. We need power, but we must learn how to control and live with it.

Quite frankly, I have very little patience with those who accuse Israel of abandoning Jewish values for reasons of political and military necessity. Statehood is a serious business and the State of Israel is not a summer camp for diaspora Jews. What are "Jewish values" held in the abstract and used to lecture others as to how to behave in dealing with the real difficulties of the human condition? It is easy to preach "Jewish values" when one does not have to pay the price.

The real question is: how do Jews preserve, foster and apply Jewish values when they must take care of themselves. When I hear my son, a medic in the Israeli tank corps who was serving in Samaria in February 1988, tell us how he saved the life of an Arab youth who wounded him in the leg and was subsequently shot in self-protection by one of my son's comrades, to me that says more about Jewish values than any number of articles on the *New York Times* Op-Ed page. In that connection, survival is also a Jewish value and it ill behooves the generation that had the good fortune to survive or not be caught up in the Holocaust to forget that.

That does not mean that there cannot be disagreements with regard to Israel's political and military policies. Israelis, like all humans, make mistakes and need to reassess matters from time to time. But there is a difference between recognizing human error and trying to correct it, and bemoaning the loss of Jewish values which seem to somehow be best preserved in a hothouse by people who do not bear the responsibility for the lives and security of others. I happen to believe that there have been few governments in history which have been so concerned with the moral aspects of their exercise of political and military power — in Israel's case, for clearly Jewish reasons, whether traditionally religious or not.

The Zionist pioneers reluctantly pursued statehood to begin with. They were reluctant to establish an army. (Indeed, the choice of the name Israel Defense Forces was designed to reflect the Zionist commitment not to have any army.) The IDF that developed spends extraordinary amounts of time — appropriately — in trying to teach its soldiers Jewish values and their practical connections with the IDF mission. We have seen some of the results of that in the IDF's recoiling from the excesses that developed out of the Arab outbreaks, a situation which by its very nature provokes excesses.

There are some who are far less attuned to these moral

dilemmas than others. There always are such in every society. And there are times when even those who are attuned will not live up to their own moral commitments. But overall, in my opinion, Israel continues to have an excellent record in this regard, one that has cost any number of Israeli lives over the years.

Despite media reports to the contrary, Israel has not lost or basically changed its sense of purpose or vision. On the most immediate level, Israel is still a place where Jews can find a secure home, where every Jew lives by right and not by sufferance, and where Jews can develop as a people and not simply as individuals. On a second level, Israel remains committed to the principle that it should be the place where the dominant culture is Jewish and where authentic Jewish cultural development — good, bad, or indifferent — is part of the life of everybody in the state (including the non-Jews), and not merely small groups of intellectuals or ultra-Orthodox. At the highest level, despite all the difficulties, Israel is still pursuing the Jewish dream of striving to become a good society, even as it strives to become a normal one.

It is this combination that sometimes goes unnoticed among Israel's critics. To be a society of saints requires that others be normal and do the saints' dirty work for them. That is the approach of those who set themselves in ivory towers, of Essenes, or Christian utopian communities. We Jews have had enough of that kind of sainthood. For us it has cost too much.

It is true that there is a tension in Zionism between the search for normality, to be like all the nations, and the effort to build a special Jewishly-informed polity — a light unto the nations. Both sides to that tension have their merits. Therefore the only way to resolve the tension between them is to try to achieve a synthesis of both, which is what Israel has been consciously or unconsciously trying to do. The big change that has taken place in the last forty years is that we are wiser now and understand that this is a more difficult task than the Zionist visionaries and those of us who followed them originally thought — in part because of the hostile environment in which Israel finds itself, in part because of the cultural baggage which we brought from the Galut, in part because of elements in the Jewish character which we conveniently could ignore as long as we were a persecuted minority and could blame them on others, and in part because of human nature in general. If the task is much harder than we thought, this only makes the challenge that much greater.

ABOUT THE AUTHORS

Gerald B. Bubis is the Alfred Gottschalk Professor of Jewish Communal Studies and the founding Director of the School of Jewish Communal Service, Hebrew Union College-Jewish Institute of Religion, Los Angeles. He is a former president of the National Conference of Jewish Communal Service, the umbrella organization for Jewish communal service in the United States. He is a vice president of the Jerusalem Center for Public Affairs and serves on the boards of the International Center for Peace in the Middle East and the New Israel Fund.

Dr. Joseph Cropsey is Distinguished Service Professor of Political Philosophy at the University of Chicago and the literary executor of the late Leo Strauss. Among his publications are *A History of Political Philosophy* (1963), of which he is co-editor with Mr. Strauss, and author of *Political Philosophy and the Issues of Politics* (1977).

Dr. Daniel J. Elazar is Senator N.M. Paterson Professor of Political Studies and Director of the Institute for Local Government, Bar-Ilan University; Professor of Political Science and Director of the Center for the Study of Federalism, Temple University; and President of the Jerusalem Center for Public Affairs. His latest book is *People and Polity: The Organizational Dynamics of World Jewry* (1989).

Dr. Gordon M. Freeman teaches political science at the Graduate Theological Union, Berkeley, California and is rabbi of Congregation B'nai Shalom in Walnut Creek. He is the author of *The Heavenly Kingdom, Aspects of Political Thought in the Talmud and Midrash* and is an Associate of the Jerusalem Center for Public Affairs.

Murray Friedman is the Mid-Atlantic States Director of the American Jewish Committee and vice chairman of the U.S. Civil Rights Commission. His latest book is *The Utopian Dilemma, American Judaism and Public Policy*, published by the Ethics and Public Policy Center.

147

Dr. Manfred Gerstenfeld is a consulting economist who resides in Jerusalem. He was one of the leaders of the Democratic Movement for Change in 1977. He is a member of the Board of Overseers of the Jerusalem Center for Public Affairs.

Dr. Robert Gordis is Professor of Bible at the Jewish Theological Seminary, editor of *Judaism*, and author of many books discussing the relationship between politics and ethics in the Jewish and other traditions.

Dr. Alfred Gottschalk is President of the Hebrew Union College-Jewish Institute of Religion and Professor of Bible and Jewish Religious Thought.

Dr. Sidney Hook is Professor Emeritus of Philosophy at City University of New York and Senior Resident Fellow of the Hoover Institute, Stanford University.

Philip M. Klutznick is one of the distinguished leaders of world Jewry. He has held many senior positions in Jewish and American public life including service as International President of B'nai B'rith, U.S. Secretary of Commerce in the Carter Administration, and former American representative to the United Nations with ambassadorial rank. In his first book, *No Easy Answers*, he has written extensively on the relationship between morality and power from the perspective of one who has been involved in some of the critical decisions of our time. He is also a member of the Board of Overseers of the Jerusalem Center for Public Affairs.

Dr. Samuel Krislov is Professor of Constitutional Law at the University of Minnesota and a frequent visiting professor in Israel. He has published extensively on constitutional problems of human rights including *The Supreme Court and Political Freedom* and *Compliance and the Law: A Multi-Disciplinary Approach*.

Judge Moshe Landau is a retired Chief Justice of the Supreme Court of Israel. As Chief Justice, he helped establish the principle of judicial review in Israeli constitutional practice. In recent years he has served as chairman of several state commissions investigating concrete problems of maintaining moral standards in Israel while it is under a state of siege.

About the Authors

Dr. Netanel Lorch is former Secretary General of the Knesset and former President of the International Association of Parliamentary Clerks. He is an Associate of the Jerusalem Center for Public Affairs, a Senior Research Fellow at Hebrew University's Truman Center, and lecturer at Bar-Ilan University.

Raquel H. Newman is a veteran Jewish communal activist and leader of the Jewish Community Federation of San Francisco, the Peninsula, Marin and Sonoma Counties. She has been involved in Israel in a variety of ways over many years and is a member of the Board of Overseers of the Jerusalem Center for Public Affairs.

Earl Raab is the retired executive director of the Jewish Community Relations Council of San Francisco and a noted commentator on civil rights, public policy and Jewish communal concerns in the United States. He is the author of *American Jewish Attitudes on Israel: Consensus and Dissent* and is an Associate of the Jerusalem Center for Public Affairs.

Rabbi Emanuel Rackman is the Chancellor and former president of Bar-Ilan University and an eminent spokesman for centrist Orthodoxy. His works on *halakhah*, philosophy, and contemporary issues are widely read.

Professor Ismar Schorsch is Chancellor of the Jewish Theological Seminary of America and, as such, principal spokesman for the World Conservative/Masorti movement. He also serves as Professor of Modern Jewish History at the JTS and is a Fellow of the Jerusalem Center for Public Affairs.

Meir Sheetrit, presently Treasurer of the Jewish Agency and the World Zionist Organization, is a former member of the Knesset and former mayor of Yavne. He is a member of the Board of Overseers of the Jerusalem Center for Public Affairs.

Max Singer, who was a founder and President of the Hudson Institute, is a professional policy analyst who lived in Israel and directed a policy research institute there from 1973 to 1977.

Dr. Bernard Susser is chairman of the Israel Political Science Association and a co-drafter of the "Constitution of Israel" proposed in 1988 by a group of Israeli academics. He is Associate

Professor of Political Studies at Bar-Ilan University, where he teaches political philosophy, and is also an Associate of the Jerusalem Center for Public Affairs. His books include *Grammer of Modern Ideology* (1988) and *Existence and Utopia: The Political Philosophy of Martin Buber* (1981).

Dr. Mervin Verbit is Professor of Sociology at Brooklyn College, a Fellow of the Jerusalem Center for Public Affairs, and a frequent commentator on American and Israeli affairs. He is co-author of *Jewishness in the Soviet Union*, among other works.

Dr. Harold Waller is Associate Professor of Political Science at McGill University, a Fellow of the Jerusalem Center for Public Affairs, and Director of the Canadian Centre for Jewish Community Studies, the Jerusalem Center's Canadian affiliate. He has written extensively on Jewish public affairs and American and Canadian public policy.

DATE DI